Wild Muse

ALSO FROM CORNERPOST PRESS

Ozarks RFD: Selected Essays (2020)
Jim Hamilton

Follow: Poems (2020)
Amy Wright Vollmar

Scattered Lights: Stories (2020)
Steve Wiegenstein

Field Trip: Stories (2022)
James Fowler

The Ballad of Johnny Bell (2022)
John Mort

Cryptozarkia (2023)
Mark Spitzer

Wild Muse

Ozarks Nature Poetry

Edited by Phillip Howerton

Cornerpost Press | 2022

ISBN: 979-8-218-06052-7

Library of Congress Control Number: 2022945400

Cover design by Phillip Howerton

Cover photo by Dennis Crider

Interior design by Phillip Howerton

Published by:
Cornerpost Press
214 West Maple
West Plains, Missouri 65775
www.cornerpostpress.com

To whippoorwills that were drawn to our doorstone; to bluegills, bullheads, and water snakes that swam in Four Mile Creek, and to milkweeds, walnut trees, and sycamores of its banks; to the toads in the dust; to cicadas, katydids, and other singers of lost summers; and to all elements of wildness that filled every crevice and moment of my childhood and have forever guarded me against loneliness and despair.

PDH

Foreword

"The comeliness of stones" is a perfect and paradoxical line in one of the poems in this collection, and I think it serves as a signal phrase for writing about the Ozarks. The natural world of the Ozarks is grand in its rewards, but those rewards come only to those who are patient and watchful, and who willingly pick through stones to see their beauty.

These poets perform that labor. The rewards are indeed grand, and as varied as the rocks at the bottom of a stream. The philosophical glints of Agnes Vojta. The loving appreciation of Amy Wright Vollmar. The evocative imagery of Phillip Howerton. The lapidary precision of John J. Han. The rich range of Wendy Taylor Carlisle. The tall-tale pyrotechnics of Mark Spitzer. The introspective navigation of Paulette Guerin. The meditative observations of C. D. Albin. The wide-ranging reflections of Gerry Sloan. The poets in this anthology bring an immense range of life experiences and poetic perspectives to their work, and each speaks in a different voice.

But one can trace threads from poet to poet, and that's where much of the delight of this anthology lies. The mysteries of Ozark rivers and springs, the ferocity of animal existence, the interplay of natural world and human interpretation — all these things recur, and rightly so. What does it mean to be an Ozarker if not to be in close contact with nature, whether one makes a living off the land or not? Even the semi-urbanites of Springfield and Bentonville navigate icy blacktop, encounter deer and possums, and listen for the wail of the tornado siren. Nature is here and now, not sometimes and elsewhere, as we try to make peace with what Hart Crane called "the old gods of the rain."

The structure of this book, in which each poet has what amounts to a chapbook's space to work in, offers the reader a particular pleasure: the ability to experience a poet at length, to experience the full range of each poet's work, and then to set that work side by side with another's. I found myself flipping back and forth in this anthology, enjoying the conversation, while at the same time appreciating the opportunity to hear each poet's voice full and clear. I thought of my childhood Wednesday night suppers in the basement of the Annapolis Presbyterian Church, full of rich dishes, everyone's finest effort, and the only regret being that one couldn't have them all in a single sitting.

So read, reflect, compare, enjoy. "With this wide wildness, these rapids and outfalls, this whooping and grinning, I overflow" is another wonderful line from this anthology, and I can't help but think it applies not just to that poet or that poem, but to the book as a whole.

Steve Wiegenstein
August 2022

Contents

The Oven Bird

Acknowledgments

About the Editor

Introduction

Almost sixty years ago I stood in the wide door of our ramshackle machine shed as winter wind slipped through cracks of its north wall, circled the dirt floor, reared its head and screamed while escaping through cracks of the south side. Only two years old, I stared, mesmerized by the wailing of the wind. I was a lucky child, for in most of my earliest memories, I am outside and encountering nature.

The poets in this collection are also lucky, for they have spent many of their creative hours engaging the natural world. Elements of nature are present in every poem. In several, nature is the central subject, as is suggested by numerous titles, such as "White-Tail," "Snow," "Turkey Buzzard," "Owl," "Old Trees," "Spring Rain," "Opossum," "Osage Orange," "The Fox," "Goggle-Eye Gobbledygook," "Ferrying Turtles," and "Crow Moon." In other poems, nature serves as a metaphor or as a presence that grants meaning to thoughts and actions of people within the poem. For example, C. D. Albin's "The Neighbor" at first appears to concentrate upon the health of a neighbor recovering from serious physical injury, but in the closing lines both men recognize the miracle of existence as they turn their eyes upon "a sky bluer, wider, / than he or I can measure." Nature in these poems, as in life, is never a passive backdrop.

As this broad engagement of nature suggests, *Wild Muse* is not a collection that merely celebrates the physical beauty of the Ozarks. Just as the poets engage numerous topics within nature, they deliver a variety of themes. Some of these poems join controversial or philosophical conversations about conservation, preservation, climate change, and anthropocentric ethics, and all of us have a duty to join these conversations and to live lightly upon this planet. These poets also recognize that they have a duty to the here and now—the duty to consider how everything large and small in nature makes our lives throb and sing. Only by being present can we experience and share the present, and only the living can do this. In *Nature* (1836), Emerson observes that "To the attentive eye, each moment of the year has its own beauty, and in the same field, it beholds, every hour, a picture which was never seen before, and which shall never be seen again." Everyone should embrace and nurture moments with nature.

Indeed, perhaps the one undeniable charge of Ozarks studies is to record our experiences in this changing place, so when it is no longer as we found it, we can bear witness to what was.

Two common interpretations of Ozarks nature are absent from this collection. Far too often it is suggested that this region still holds a pristine wilderness and that its natural beauty is indestructible. Such views are understandable, for, when compared to many other regions, the Ozarks appears to have a wealth of green space and clean water. Such depictions are incomplete, unrealistic, and pernicious, for it is convenient and reassuring to believe wildness still exists and nature cannot be destroyed. Such comfortable views can lull us into complacency. The poets in *Wild Muse* are grounded enough in Ozarks history to know that the fabled forest primeval was long ago lost to the timber industry, that much of the ground water has been compromised, and that many of our streams are chert-filled and shallow shadows of their former selves.

As Steve Wiegenstein notes in the foreword, this chapthology presents a generous helping of poems from each writer, granting a sense of each poet's range while allowing the freedom to create conversations by juxtaposing poems and poets. Edsel Ford, a poet from northern Arkansas, opens the discussions with "Return to Sunday Creek" in which the narrator returns to a favorite natural place of his past and finds it reduced and damaged. His themes of sense of place, appreciation of beauty, and loss and responsibility run through the heart of *Wild Muse*. In the closing poem, Robert Frost's "The Oven Bird," the bird, who has witnessed the passing of summer and the withering of nature, ponders "what to make of a diminished thing." It is hoped that readers will be inspired to join these conversations—and perhaps write some poems of their own in response.

PDH

"Nature is the vehicle of thought."

Ralph Waldo Emerson
Nature, 1836

Return to Sunday Creek

There are no quiet places now:
No deeps. Where once the willow bough
Dipped onto water still and green.
Six feet deep and so serene
You couldn't guess what worlds were there,
A twisted stump leans on the air.

You were a boy then: let it go.
Perhaps it wasn't really so . . .
Perhaps the curve beneath the bluff
Was shallow then, ran swift. Enough.
The silk-shod snake beside the stream
Is smaller now. So is the dream.

Take care, however, lest returning
Again, you find the river burning.

Edsel Ford
Arkansas Poet, 1928-1970

C. D. Albin

White Oak
Quercus alba

C. D. Albin

I am a native Ozarker, born in West Plains, Missouri, the same town where I returned after graduate school to make my home and begin teaching at Missouri State-West Plains, a two-year, open-admission campus.

Returning home was not my plan when I left for college, but after choosing to major in English, I found myself most drawn to those writers who grappled with their rural and small-town roots. Fiction writers like William Faulkner, Ernest J. Gaines, and Willa Cather seemed to be writing just for me. Later, when I returned to graduate school at the University of Mississippi, the Louisiana novelist and short story writer Tim Gautreaux convinced me that I had something to say, and that it could be said through stories about my people and my region.

Later still, I attended a reading on my own campus featuring the poet Matthew Brennan, a fellow Missourian who was on the English faculty at Indiana State University. Although I had never thought seriously about writing poetry, I came away from Matt's reading compelled to try, and so began a second literary apprenticeship. I owe direct debts to both Tim and Matt, whose examples and encouragement made possible my first two books, *Hard Toward Home: Stories*, and *Axe, Fire, Mule: Poems*. I'm most grateful, and always will be.

I never took a poetry writing class in college or graduate school. I was more interested in fiction writing, so I let good opportunities slip by. When I did begin trying to write poems, I learned by reading poets like Matt Brennan, Walt McDonald, Ted Kooser, and the late Claudia Emerson. Then I began to read two poets, Ron Rash and Gary Fincke, whose commitment to syllabic poetry deeply influenced me. I liked the discipline of writing syllabic lines, largely because doing so required a precision with language that improved both my poetry and fiction.

Of the poets mentioned above, McDonald and Rash are especially beholden to the natural world, McDonald to the Staked Plains region around Lubbock, Texas, and Rash to the Appalachian Mountains of the western Carolinas. In their work I was able to see how I might represent my own region, the Ozarks, in my poetry. Each writer evokes his landscape in great detail, but each is also concerned about the people who live their lives in, with, and sometimes against that landscape.

The land I know best is the land my father purchased in the 1950s, with the dream of starting a Quarter Horse farm. Decades later I built my home on a portion of that land, siting the house on a ridge beneath a canopy of oak, hickory, and cedar. I find that living in a place I have known since birth, a place I have walked in all seasons and glimpsed from every angle, influences my poetry immeasurably. I would likely be a very different poet without this place. Possibly I would not be a poet at all.

Here and Now

Man brings all things to the test of himself,
and this is notably true of lightning.
Aldo Leopold

Sawdust scrim settles as he
sinks the chainsaw deep within

a fallen trunk, makes quick work
of an oak even lightning

took a year to kill. Last spring,
when night bolts lit the hollow,

a jolt of sound pounded his
ear drums, bounced him to his feet

beside his bed and left him
wandering in full dark, his

own house a mazy box built
by strangers. No Leopold

counting rings, he looks ahead
to months of dry oak burning

in his stove, bullying winds
bluffing beneath eaves. His creed—

let pretend farmers ponder
past as prologue. He serves here

and now, does what needs doing
to keep lights on, his house warm.

White-Tail

At night they mat orchard grass
to flat ovals, browse garden
rows by dawn, till the back door

claps behind me and springing
haunches launch them beyond tilled
soil toward viney green walls of

understory—fleet crashing
of hoof, leaf, limb—then the long
day's silence of their going.

Intruder

Sunday noon, hiking an old
trail behind the house, I catch
something at the farthest edge

of vision, and turning, find
the owl already turned—head
swiveled on drought-brown body,

its claw-perch a corner post.
You, I think, and remember
porch evenings, flinch of my

own flesh at the screech, the rip
in the airy cloth of night,
though no night is here, only

blank, noiseless distance between
its eye and mine, until I
lean an inch too far, dislodge

a stone and startle eons
of instinct that spur the bird
to heavy, shadow-stalked flight.

Burial Oak

They dropped the lightning-struck tree
where the acorn had fallen,

burying brute stump and ball
among roots thick as saplings,

rings so contracted by drought
they were left to guess at age.

He supposed he could have sold
such stout abundance of wood

to any man standing there,
winter so soon coming on,

but judged he owned a duty
as roughly equal in worth.

Late that fall the oak warmed him
on land where they'd each had birth.

The Subterfuge of Stones

Near campus, an old man kept
a store of stones he had sawn
in two, sanding, polishing,
until veins of minerals
swirled brighter than rainbow bands.
Each afternoon he opened
his door to offer lessons
in the subterfuge of stones,
their abraded surfaces
camouflaging the beauty
he uncovered at their core.

Homesick for horses and hills,
I possessed little patience
when he romanticized rocks
like those I'd hauled all summer
from my father's fields, tossing
them like trash, piles rising high
as my head by season's end.

Diamonds in the rough, he'd say,
when I mentioned the labor
I hated, the monuments
of stones I had abandoned.
His smile was all tolerance
each time I returned to class,
cocksure my fortune would need
to be made, mustered, not found
in some comeliness of stones.

The Cellar

Pungency of must lingers
when I lift the cellar door,
descend stone steps wedged in earth
a decade after raiders
made terror their currency,
emptying the countryside
of neighbors they'd left bereft
of home and kin regardless
of fealty or uniform.
Now those stairs lead into dank
darkness, until the light cord
skims my shoulder and I pull,
revealing rows of fruit jars
hoarded against certain need
by descendants of those who
burrowed here like creatures, hewed
stone on which I'd one day stand.

Notice of Sale

Laminated now, a frayed notice hangs
from a back wall in my mother's basement—
printed evidence of a farm still called
the home place to this day, although the sale
was transacted a century ago.

Firmly, we decree point of origin
from the near past, electing to ignore
Derbyshire, or the two generation
sojourn in County Meath, or a hamlet
in north Virginia bearing our surname.

We choose instead a swath of Ozark soil—
scant of loam, bestrewn by stone—to ordain
our beginning even though the land leant
sparse nurture, and five of seven children
sought hope of solace in rumored elsewheres.

Last fall the youngest passed at eighty-six
in Literberry, Illinois, five hours
north of natal soil he revisited
every other year, reuniting
with kin to tell, then retell tales of home.

His absence severed the eroding chain
of porch bards who knew the farm as children,
boundaries marked by barbed wire and cedar,
until they learned venturing beyond meant
gain and loss, same as any trade or sale.

Provenance

Stone points lie under glass, affixed to felt,
more than one hundred arrowheads bequeathed
by my father, who believed they were claimed

from the floors and ledges of Ozark caves.
The points are cached in an upstairs closet
where I rarely disturb them, too aware

of their doubtful provenance to shoulder
unburdened possession, yet I covet
the skill to read precise parings of stone,

decipher the force of an artisan's
striking hand, antique, flint-wrought testament
to whom these shapely points should be returned.

The Osage seem likely—Ozark legends
forced from Missouri hills to Kansas plains,
murdered for headrights in Oklahoma.

Their families were riven by absence,
memories torn like discarded remnants
of a doll chain, scissored wisps suggesting

still discernible shapes of the missing.
But what mending might stores of heirloom stones
achieve beyond the serrated solace

of the tangible, the prick-point piercings
in clenched fist? From this safe distance I pray
for balm, although my home crowns a hilltop

Osage yielded two centuries ago—
an obdurate fact predestined to wound
like the chiseled point of an arrowhead.

Origin Stories

Like images engraved upon both sides
of a coin, the historical marker
outside the Ozark Heritage Center

tells dual tales of hometown history.
Facing west, the marker greets visitors
with a narrative of modest founding,

Josephus Howell having thought to open
a post office inside his home, circa
1850. The Civil War requires

a separate paragraph to recount
rebels who fled Union troops, and raiders
who burned the town in 1863,

resettlement impeded for two years.
Facing east, the marker's back side informs
the reader of an ancient north-south trail

running through the county and alleges
more than a thousand prehistoric mounds
remain in the region. The town resides

in territory Osage vacated
in 1808, although the Shawnee
and Delaware continued to visit

through 1840. Highway 63,
now running north-south across the county,
assails the Ozark Heritage Center

with incessant sounds of passage, drivers
flinging road grit at sixty miles per hour,
the peppered ditches tracing their absence.

The Neighbor

I come upon him trimming
a large pin oak that anchors

the final bend in his drive,
surprised he'll chance harm again

so soon after therapy
for a brain battered and bruised

by a plummeting pine bough.
His forearms strain with the weight

of the saw, resisting rest
until I commend his health,

swear he looks hale as ever.
Lowering the tool, he sags

like an empty sack. *So blessed
to be here*, he keens, peeking

at a sky bluer, wider,
than he or I can measure.

Testament

I'm twelve and they are watching,
old people with soft faces and fleshy smiles,
their gray heads bobbing approval.

A fat man holds one hand above the water,
his arm hairs gilded by the sun.
His thick fist pulls me close,

flattens on my forehead as if feeling
for fever. Old words slur near my ear,
rays ricochet across the sky, and I'm plunged

so deep my fingers sink into silt.
The force of my rising belongs to him,
my limbs hapless as I break the surface

and slosh back toward the bank,
dripping water into water, smelling of fish.

Glaucoma

Field test, the nurse calls this tiresome task,
me clicking away at pin dots of light
that blip on the screen, or straining to spot

faint afterglows, my thumb a jumpy
trigger finger. *Stay with me,* she urges,
concerned that I catch every burst

of fool's gold passing through
my field of vision, but I need no test
to see the field is shrinking, darkness

closing in. When I was nine the night
would fall like that, sneaking from all sides
until the hayfield where I played

was scarcely wider than my reach,
fireflies lighting moments narrower
than breath, but never the way home.

Ozark Dark

Most nights I wake to cacophonies
of coyotes in the near pasture,
high pitched yips following a frenzy

of kill-lust, bellies filled with rabbits,
mice, maybe a luckless barn cat—then
silence sudden as a snake strike. Soon

come bedeviled bays from our Bluetick
ranging in caged torment along the
fenced ridgetop, his howls drifting heartsick

over the hollows. Weary, I shift
weight to stare at the window, ponder
lamentations of the Ozark dark.

Pharaoh Dreamed of Cattle

Rucked acres ripple south toward
Arkansas, Herefords dotting

dry pastures grazed to stubble
that crunches under hooves. We've

been months with no rain, high sky
unbroken except for sun

and buzzards day after day.
Pharaoh dreamed of fat cattle

rising from the river Nile
to feast on green grass, until

others came, thin-flanked ones like
mine, so hungry they ate those

ready for market, startling
Pharaoh from his sleep. These steamed

nights, sweating through sheets, I think
I would welcome some seer

from another land, Joseph
able to cull my fevered

dreams, pronounce the yea or nay
of seasons. Instead, I hear

the reedy drone of insects
beyond the window, or the

sudden yips of coyotes
as they surround some lone thing

caught apart from its nest, hole,
hidden den. Come morning, I

often find small bones flashing
white in the sun. With boot toe

I sift them, play at reading
bone for sign, until bawling

cattle send me to the barn,
where I load leavings of last

summer's hay, dry wind drifting
straw across dirt like tinder.

Cicero Jack, Farmer,
Rues the Ruin of an Ozark River

They might as well track clay mud
on my great-aunt's Persian rug,
beer-swilling week-enders down
from Springfield or St. Louis,
hell-bent to float a clear stream
where they swear litter laws don't
apply and local accents
prove inbreeding. Yesterday
I watched one fool stand and whiz
till he flipped his hooting friends
face first into the current,
their aluminum canoe
upended while they waded,
wobbling and cursing, toward the
near bank. *Watch for moccasins*
I called to one drunk sloshing
beneath limbs, but he stared back
as if I'd sprouted a horn
from my forehead. That's when I
left them to serpents as their
natural kin. But later,
my truck stalled in the middle
of Brixey Bridge, I spotted
their stone-stoved canoe adrift
in swift water. My heart kicked
like the time I came upon
a thrown rider down Devil's
Backbone, and old as I am
I shinnied that bank praying
my body would muster strength
to rescue what I could. The
canoe cradled only shoes,
an Orvis cap, and empties
of Coors and Busch. Knee deep or
better, river rock rolling
beneath my feet, I wrestled

the whole mess to dry ground, scanned
that noon-bright surface until
hyena giggles carried
over the water to tell
me they'd survived, would return
to weekday suits, paisley ties.

The Will and Testament of Cicero Jack

From this porch I can scan the same ridges
my father did, be proud I've kept them clear
of crowded subdivisions that bear such

names as Quail's Nest or Fox Run, where people
pass lives I cannot understand, their land
diced down to fractions of a single

acre, their sunsets blocked by neighbors' roofs.
Two weeks ago in Tulsa I stood at
the window of a great-grandson's room, saw

twenty feet of backyard and wondered where
he'd find space to run, or whether being
boxed in on every side by tract houses

of identical brick would still-birth all
his bodily ambition. I know
I'm an old man with hardened ways, stubborn

beyond sense in the eyes of kin, but if
I could pronounce my clear will to the world
and have it heard, I'd defend that boy's right

to pace his own days, not have his living
sped up just to double the jingle in
someone else's pocket. That Tulsa tract

betokens business beyond my span
of years, hints at the windfall hopes of heirs
who wish this farm converted to bass boats

and bank accounts. One day their wants are sure
to win, but not while I breathe. A man can
live no testimony other than his

own, the inside of his story the one
possession he can never bequeath,
the tale he must clasp bone-close in the grave.

Cicero Jack Considers the Cougar's Return

When we came to this valley
there were a good many panthers in the mountains.
                    Theodore Pease Russell

They took the last cat the year I was born,
some lone survivor stalking boggy backwaters
of the bootheel. I imagine him crouched

in the fork of trunk and limb, a tawny ball
growling down on the dogs before the bullet
battered his brain, darkening all. Somewhere

a photo shows his carcass stretched at the feet
of stern-faced hunters, their rifles lined like
fence posts. A decade later, hill men still told

old tales learned from grandfathers, and I grew
taller listening to firelight voices lift in pitch
when panther lore storied the night. If you

hear one past dark, they'd say, you'll think
some woman's screaming for life, or they'd
picture pioneers down on the White or Buffalo,

men who would legend themselves hunting
yellowed eyes by torchlight, or sometimes
tangling hand and knife before stumbling away

half alive, their gazes fixed to distant ridges.
I've passed more than eighty years on such tales,
no fondness for rumors of cougars that

managed to ghost Ozark creek bottoms
or cragged overlooks without leaving a track,
a scrape, a pile of their own scat. But now

comes this year of proof—young males shot
by ranchers or caught on film by trail cameras,
one scarcely half a mile away.

Conservation agents say they're moving
out of Nebraska, maybe South Dakota,
wanderers scouting new territory, inspiring

paranoia when backyard pets turn up dead.
I know the difference between a coyote's kill
and something more, but still ponder why

I've taken to my porch these last few nights,
listening for something other than the bark
of dogs or bawl of cattle. I've caught

the swooped flush of owl's wings, awakened—
startled—to the faint, near-dawn chittering
of smaller things, but mostly I hear the

rattle-hiss of my own night breath, systole,
diastole, the heart's stubborn memory:
they took the last cat the year I was born.

Axe, Fire, Mule

Last summer the banks of my
pond bore hoof scars where cattle
lumbered down to stand hock-deep
in drought dregs and drink. Now crops

rot beneath constant cloudspill
while I watch brown water wash
across land my grandfather
cleared with axe, fire, mule. Heart raw,

I work hours in soaked boots, ask
how water can be mock of
God one day, print of his hand
the next. Maybe old Noah

knew, but nothing's sure for me
except Julie and the kids
need all that's left of us here.
We'll stay, start over—rain, shine.

Wendy Taylor Carlisle

Eastern Redbud
Cercis canadensis

Wendy Taylor Carlisle

Wendy Taylor Carlisle was born in Manhattan, grew up in Florida, received an MA in history at the University of Arkansas-Fayetteville and an MFA in writing from Vermont College of Union Institute in 2003. She has been briefly a songwriter, a waitress, a bartender, a band manager, a secretary, an editor at the *Arkansas Territorial Restoration*, a lecturer/grad assistant/ library assistant and for the past 30 years a writer, mostly of poetry. Her first glimpse of the Ozarks was in 1973 when she passed through Eureka Springs on her way to Colorado. She saw Colorado, turned right around, and came back to Arkansas and now lives in a house she began building in 1980 and hasn't finished yet.

She is the author of four books, *Reading Berryman to the Dog* (2000), *Discount Fireworks* (2008), *On the Way to the Promised Land Zoo* (2019), and *The Mercy of Traffic* (2019), for which she received the 2020 Phillip H. McMath Post-Publication Award. Her chapbooks include *After Happily Ever After*, *Persephone on the Metro*, *They Went Down to the Beach to Play*, and *Chap Book*. Her work has appeared in several anthologies including *The Poets Grimm* (2003), *Drawn to Marvel* (2014), *Untold Arkansas: An Anthology* (2018), and *Fiolet and Wing: An Anthology of Domestic Fabulist Poetry* (2019).

She has been nominated for the Pushcart Prize thirteen times and has been twice nominated for best of web. Doubleback Books reprinted her 2008 book, *Discount Fireworks* in 2020. See some of her poems online and in print in *Persimmon Tree*, *pacificREVIEW*, *2RiverView*, *Kentucky Review*, *Cider Press Review*, *Lost River Review*, *Mom Egg*, *barzakh*, *San Pedro River Review*, *Atlanta Review*, *Freshwater Review*, *Tab*, and *Rattle*. Her website is www.wendy taylorcarlisle.com.

She writes: I live on the backside of a mountain, down a dirt road. I have a husband and two dogs. The dogs keep the deer out of the tulips. My husband keeps my spirits up. We have a neighbor who appears in a lot of my poems. He grows tomatoes. We all eat.

In the morning the sun washes up the hollow and lights the scraggly oaks that blunder into daylight. At sunset, the heat goes out of the mountains in a hurry and the fireflies—what there are left of them—rise out past the gravel pile where the forest begins in a tangle of kudzu, brush, and third-growth trees. Other humans are scarce.

The poems in this collection reflect the quiet way we live, although the silence on this hillside is not silence at all. It is the sound of leaf rustle, branch creaking, and critters, their grunts, yips, trills, and whistles. While writing and living, I always remember that I am just a hiccup in the woods, an interruption to the fox and possum, deer and raccoon.

I peer from my room, out south of town, near where a committee of vultures rests and listen as rumors blow into the leaves. The news gets around; therefore, I know some things. Also, I don't know some things. Whatever happens, I have a peculiar turn of mind.

I write poetry because prose confuses me, because my head fills up with rhyme, because poetry susurrates and moans and sighs and whispers and sings at my shoulder. Poetry because it is in every corner, around every dogleg turn, because it is dilemma and euphoria. Poetry because without poetry, what?

One of my favorite writing axioms comes from Ta-Nehisi Coates, "Talent is important, but perseverance and high threshold for humiliation is maybe even more important."

The first poem that follows is my answer to that often-asked question, "Where do you get your inspiration?"

Inspiration

Don't panic. The answer's simple really,
beautiful and slick as a California seal.
It lies there on a flat rock just off the coast
smelling of fish and salt. Survey it.

Pause to admire the sockeye's ivory belly,
the mahi-mahi's flashing gills.
Watch for the gull's red legs, then
ease into your own cold tide. Paddle

straight out to where anchovy,
those little silver knives, school past
your ashy knees. Clutch a favorite poem
like a child's striped float and wait

for the muse in a bright red speedo.
As she strokes past, let her splash you.

Rumor

To write about Ozark summer you have to have the animal memory of swelter, of low water, of dry sumps, of deer come close to the cow pond, of cattle down to the lick log, of NO BURN signs everywhere. You have to remember Twenty-Twelve, the second hottest year on record or Nineteen Fifty-Six, which by word of mouth, was the first. But this summer I'm writing about was the worst summer since Satan fell, or so we thought. The cities simmered to a boil in their tarmac, bubbling down to heat stroke. Everywhere preachers promised Armageddon like always and used one hundred and ten degrees for proof.

With no air condition, it was too hot to make love even with fans at the head and foot of the bed making a middle turbulence. We couldn't move after noon or sleep before midnight. How many hours can a person spend at Harts pushing a wire cart through the cans and bottles—15 minutes to choose a sponge, a half hour for a soft drink that only stays chilled straight out of the cooler box? Winter was a rumor that summer hid under each overheated scarp. We searched for anything cold and hid what we found.

It may be that we were brown and swam it. It may be when we could, we stepped down from the cliff into the icy river water imagining ourselves Cherokee just passing through or Quapaw or settlers who learned long ago to make some peace with the heat. Let's just say the weather sweated us and we got no relief from those jumped-up preachers.

August: An Ozark Sonnet

August, ripe as a peach, convinces us / there's still time for travel.

August holds on by a fingernail / as summer fails.

August feels hotter because of accretion and span. / July is hotter by the numbers.

August trees have grown dusty / in air thick and sweet as taffy.

August outshines the previous sultry. / Its wind rouses your nose to what's coming.

August reports back from fecundity central. / Report shows harvest to follow.

August is the fading profile on a worn coin. / Summer is that coin, vanishing.

Cuts

Larry cuts stone in a humming cloud of birds.
It is hot. He is calm. The birds are hungry.

They zoom around him as the patio emerges
from a jumble of rock. How does he do it?

Patiently, carefully, with string and level.
I am confounded by this skill, being an expert

in the surface cut only, in splinter removal,
in the self-inflicted wound. Larry's saw drones

while my husband feeds the hummingbirds,
tiny blast furnaces. Sugar and water,

sugar and water disappear down their ruby throats
all through the hot months. Larry works

patiently, week into week, finishes,
packs his chisels and leaves. Fall is fewer than

ten days away and we think the birds should
be gone with the season. Under our breath,

we urge them to fly as they buzz the windows,
not ready to leave their just-paved patio.

One morning we fill the feeders
for what we promise ourselves will be the last time,

forgetting how the hummingbirds stunned us,
circling Larry's head like a crown.

Come and Gone: An Ozark Sonnet

Big summer bugs thud / against the curtainless windows, suicides

for last light after the day / has poured out its bucket of shine.

Fireflies harry the still-green leaves. / Oh Lord of Come and Gone,

let me be stunned / by these final days of summer

as the sun recasts its slant, / a breeze blows in, gravid with fall.

Let me be capable of feeling / this new season's chill promise.

Let me be like the leaf, / momentary in fire, content to be lost.

Ode

Ripened and blessed for another season,
in late heat we haven't lit a fire yet, although
the first frost's been and gone along the ridge
and brought the trees to peak. Wasps stir and blunder
into second summer, flies trouble the screens
and garden gourds dry on a windowsill.
We welcome any whippoorwills' *whip will—will—will*
that echoes in the vaporish timber where every squirrel
has been transformed into a sleek, full-coated garden lord
and all the acres call us to our knees in a rapture of mulch
and bulb to turn the ground again beside the creek.

Each dawn gives up its cirrus sky, and weak light
Scrapes the oaks and stalks across the pines,
While acorns underfoot crack like buckshot
In the piled-up leaves. A doe, keen with fall rut,
Leaps to the two-lane, takes the headlights in.

How could I wish for trickster spring
when an October morning skitters through the yard,
the cider runs down, sweet and pale and afternoon
lights up the tin shed roof? What could I relish more
than geese to honk the hill awake on their way south?
A hunter's moon raises an orange sign.
If friends sing somewhere else, what does that matter?
Fall is the shelter before the heart winters over.

Naked

The fall your father died all the leaves came down
in a three-day rainstorm. It was a damned fine storm.
The rain went on steady, one day into the next, while
the leaves fell slow and constant, regular as rain-drops.

The last hay baled weeks before, farmers at the co-op
had nothing to do but nod and rock and spit, and watch
the trees strip 'til they were naked against the carpeted fields.

You were thirty-four the year those wet hills unrolled, glossy
as a calendar picture, and you took your father's cancer
like you did the weather. Under the dripping eaves, your chair
tipped back, you talked about the hay, but you seemed lighter,

more like a boy, as if your father's passing gave you back
childhood, stripped you, washed you down. As if he fathered you,
dying, and you could be naked then, being his son.

Smudged

There's a doe dead on the roadside, a grille sacrifice. "Rut gets them and they jump right at you," says Larry, who knows about deer and also the coons here although I haven't glimpsed one, or the big buck from the hollow either, since the dogs came to live with us. I've seen an armadillo, though, shuffling away to mine the brush, her scythe claws at the roots.

This afternoon, rain steams the pasture. The big dog shakes his collar. A flea-lean fox spooks her kit across the new blacktop on 1080. Walking, we came on a mountain lion den in the cliffs, a lice-eaten carcass above the dry stream and shed antlers everywhere. Summer was supposed to end today. The forecast for rain then chill, swelter ushered out. Instead, a hot spell squats in the woods where nothing stirs but invisible game.

Yesterday the Lomi Lomi masseur cleansed my friend's place. He used a hawk fan, an eagle bone flute, a fresh-water turtle shell, sage, and sweetgrass. During the ceremony, copal-smoke nosed the corners of her rooms. Once he cleansed her house, the *kumu* cleansed my friend. She said her whole life changed at that moment, but there's still no break in the weather. Hot September squats in the woods, stalled in heat-thick air and cicadas churr. I figure it was a too-small space the Lomi Lomi guy smudged, not nearly big enough to scrub the mountain, not wide enough to bring on real rain and that gratifying chill. No cool today, only the usual sweat and animal rustle.

Weather

Out the window, a grey morning—
the trees urge to bud but show no leaves.

There's a furtive rumble of grievance
in the mountains. Hard politics

and a jitter of future drought,
a wonder of gravel bars in the lake.

Grocery prices rise and well-meaning
neighbors polish their guns.

Could it be that this year winter missed us?
We anticipate late snow

as, behind the hedge, spring kills time,
whips up a broken-egg wind.

NEST: An Ozark Sonnet

Let us gladly pile up leaves and fall in them. / Let us unpack sheepskin boots

weeks before we need them and / be deep in chill before we understand

what's happened to summer. / Let the season be a subtle wound

on our skin as it pales and we finish / the last of the fresh basil and begin

a marinara with this year's home-canned tomatoes. / Oh, let us be confused by losing an hour

and scratched by wool socks / and please, let us be concerned more

with a warm nest than with how helpless / we will be against the cold.

Catch and Release

The birds fly out,
the wind begins.   The wind flies out,
the birds retreat and moonlight
sings in your rowdy mouth.

                    The rain leans in
to snow behind the window glass
and all up on the ridge
the outside worries to be let in.

                    The cat's gone to the fox,
and the carpenter with the ruined ankles
grieves all our losses.
Chapter and verse, he says,
catch and release, it's all the same.

The moon goes dark. The moon flies out.
The broken-legged wind goes flat,
                    the cold and dark begin.

Cold Time: An Ozark Sonnet

This is the time of year for downed timber, / for seeing through the trees where trailer houses

mushroomed this past summer. Plodding / through chill afternoons, we come on

Indian currant by the trail, a shock of pink / berries chilled to mauve, bird fodder

to the end of winter, past the scarred elder / where a yearling buck rubbed velvet off

his new antlers. We make out cherry logs, / fresh chopped and pumpkin orange at the cut.

Galls on the oak are eggshell-thin, wasps gone. / This is the cold time, rain crow flown

whose stutter calls out storms. We urge the last / persimmon from its branch and find it rotten.

Spell: An Ozark Sonnet

The coyotes cry on the hillside, / their yip, eerie as the world before

the first word, a river of noise, / a babble that seems to boil

from inside my ear, so deep / in my skull that it becomes

a voice chiding, or one reading / a beloved book, wrapping itself

around the long surrounding, / darkness, outside and in,

until that voice, which is my / woods-memory and also an oracle,

settles itself into instructions / becomes a living spell.

Snow

The late cold slips in at toe-level where the door
isn't quite flush, dragging more cold behind,
and rain becoming snow
that unpacks sweaters with lost buttons,
the ones that sprung an elbow hole
or grew a matted fake fur collar,
sweaters destined for Goodwill, but not quite yet.
April chill, the surprise we had to survive.
In a house with a bedroom in the cellar
built into the hillside where our now-lost son
slept like a stored turnip under his frost-rimmed window
while we played blues day and night as if those
flatted fifth notes could warm us or ward off the snow
that was coming, the snow we knew would come.

Buck Mountain

Before the rain, I couldn't imagine the rain.
It is that way with me. Yesterday, I filled with brilliant
sunlight, with air faintly green, reflecting
the everything that rises in spring. Yesterday

was dry and so forever is dry. Around here, the Kings River
runs clean as it can. Eagles rise against the bluffs,
a canoe snakes, loops, slides sweet up to Clifty.
In any weather I am a forecast atheist.

Torrents come as a surprise, boil the creek with runoff,
pulse the flannel hillside light with crows,
riding the breeze like oil on water. I float in vitreous air,
contained by ignorance and caws.

Warnings are nothing to me. A momentary drought
the creek clear again, how can I believe the glass will ever break?

Undress

There's no way to turn off the days' lengthening,
no way to stop the gnats gathering like dust

against the backdoor or the late moths stacked
around the porch light's slanted shine.

This is the season that loses night, an outgrown
black sleeve showing off a pallid wrist.

It arrives stinking of new weeds and frog spawn.
You can't resist the bob and blow of its standard weathers,

the breeze and shower that decorate
their beds with tulip, the sodden soil with daffodil.

Erratic as trout, spring days won't lie flat.
They glisten and slide, rise up, slap their tails on a planked dock,

flip back in, slow to quit the pond's thaw and sloppy ease.
Take in a lungful of the season. Undress for months.

OK to Burn

After the two hours it took to turn her to four pounds of grit,
as the box of her waits on a shelf for what might be a funeral

but turns instead into a trek by the Buffalo River,
April-riled and moiling, bridge-high at Steele Creek,

scouring the cliffs—Big Bluff and Rock Bluff—
past the abandoned cooler of Schlitz at Kyles Landing,

past the Elk Museum at Ponca and into the Boxley Valley
by the Arkansas Hotel, the Little Buffalo running at the back,

pale Kiss-Me-by-the-Gate on its ruined arbor, through
spongy hills, the burn ban lifted everywhere in Madison County,

signs on the firehouses: *OK to Burn* in Alabam and *OK* in Kingston
and Marble Falls, where all down to Jasper, the fields are overrun

with primrose, daisy in the ditches, the pastures ripe with pulsing
yellow Coreopsis named here Tickseed, the foliage favoring

a second-green, the one she used to call chartreuse, the dogwood
still undistracted by blossom, everywhere iris rampaging

in purple and peach, sandy wild strawberries that hint of coming
summer, pink as the inside of a lover's lip, Egyptian

Walking Onions creeping, the hay fields burgeoning as the grey
translucence of her ashes lifts over the hillside like blown gauze.

Bees

When Larry's Garden begins the work of burgeoning
it has no more memory of last fall's turned earth
than smolder has of fire, but plants begin to push

and reach, with the smallest stem, and bees arrive
with the blossoms, their work, the work of plant-making,
the labor of hum, unconditional, relational. Later,

there will be catnip, *Nepeta cataria,* to pull
for the lions and tigers at the wild animal sanctuary
up the road where interns in identical khaki

stuff it into pillowcases for the big cats to roll on,
but even with the joyous lions and the bees'
hard labor, there's a way to travel from muck

to vegetables and I must imagine Larry's harvest,
the way a stream imagines its future canyon.

Kings River

How on the river my eye grows fierce, making a new world
in this fast-running canoe, prisoner of the season,

full of it, mouth wide open, shouting, barely able to catch
a breath, stunned by canyon and cliff

and their enchantments. How this river dumbfounds me
with its harsh beauty, its terrifying splendor.

There must be ugly rivers somewhere with jagged
trashed shores, where I could be comfortable, floating

on the stagnant water among the plastic bags and beer cans,
next to a sullen companion I'd grown used to.

But oh, with this wide wildness, these rapids and outfalls,
this whooping and grinning, I overflow.

Blossom

"... old in a blossoming earth" Robert Creeley

In the south of my childhood, time passed
like a plate of ham. Grandma made lard biscuits,

cooked rashers of bacon, fried pork chops,
presided over the hugging and sassing

and eating and telling and pulling of sticker burrs.
I looked to her for solace and solutions. She delivered

axioms and injunctions and was indifferent to the one,
strong chin hair that grew and when pulled, grew again,

unkillable as a cockroach. How and why
do a woman's eyebrows grow both thin and wild?

In the south of my childhood, we knew our place
and kept it until, like grandma our strength of hand

declined to loss of grip as the silverware tumbled
from our fingers like petals from a blossoming limb.

We Walk the Trail More Slowly

The two limping men and I adjust our speed

to the newest buds, the serviceberry,

called here "sarvis," bloomed and blown,

its leaves beginning, the chartreuse red bud starts,

knots that will be dogwood blossoms.

We are old and interested in world news

and local gossip, and in the carpet of henbane

on Larry's yard, and wood frogs and tree frogs

chirping by the cow pond. Spring

begins again, just as it always has, and we

are here together, watching effulgence unfold.

Dream

In Dreams we are everything in the room. . . .
Chinua Achebe

In the nights when I still dreamed, I dreamed I was a farmer, dreamed as a farmer I mean. The chickens (me), goats, (me) in a dreamy rain. I ran after the molting biddies (also me) in their gray mourning feathers to remind them (a group of me) we should stop laying.

The dream had me-moths that live a day then die, had a forgotten retablo of me, had my Ozark hive mind, had me, an Arkansas armadillo, on her back bloating, (yes me) even as far north as where I am now, plus a casino (me) with a casino dog (also me), her paws (mine) like demitasse saucers.

I woke that morning in my own bed with the same bedpost as always and the same memories and peered out over the toes I was sure were mine. I woke in the glory of hummingbirds, horseflies, field iris and dogwood, oak, pine and rock scattered on thin soil. I woke to an unintentional fern garden, the slope painted with qualities of green, with fox skitter, blades of light that slash into the brush and crows to mishandle the phone wire.

I woke with my hillside outside tamed into my glade, with my pastures, woke with the knowledge that the woods will reclaim all that is mine when the toes I stare over are gone.

Turkey Buzzard

They are like gods in the trees, the vultures.
We call them turkey buzzards, although they are neither.

They would be regal if they weren't so ugly, or maybe
they are ugly and regal, like the Hapsburgs,

whose family name comes from high German
for hawk castle, but hawks are hunters

and our vultures are weak-footed scavengers.
You see how I did that, gathered up the vultures

into our family like that, acknowledging
what they are in the air, our flying kettle,

the local clean-up crew for confused tourists
mistaking armadillos for garbage on the road, unable

to dodge the doe launching herself from the verge,
for hunters who abandon what's left

of butchered deer carcasses back in the scrub—
dogs first, then vultures at the bones—

our uglies who come back to roost in the pasture oak.
Resting like that, they are properly called a committee

but when they feed, the vultures like vengeful deities
are known as a wake.

Provision

my friend feeds rats to a hawk

rat catchers come to her house

and trap the rats in cages and kill them

then she carries the rat cages to the reservoir

and holds the rats up by their tails

for the hawk to swoop down and seize them

and miraculously the hawk comes

she is brave to do that, I think

so close to a raptor's heartbeat, to the wing

that could put out her eye or knock her down

and I envy the joy of that wildness so close

and imagine her wind-blown hair and her

standing firm and the hawk approaching

Up Here We Make Our Own Darkness

First light dallies with the walnuts and pine on the lip of land
that drops to a hollow I admit I'll never explore.

I circle. I peer through the trees as the dogs crash down, but I don't
walk the creek bed. I'm afraid of the slope.

Could be because of arrowheads, broken pots, and the spirits of Americans
whose names I can only guess. Larry says Quapaw,

but surely not the Hitchiti, whose true name, *A'tcik hå'ta*, was swallowed by
the Muskogee, although other First Nations passed through and left behind

their ghosts and footprints, their cries and chants and children's bones.
Maybe I shy away because of the bones, or the panther Game and Fish

swear isn't here, the one that trailed Larry home after he stumbled
into its den and poked around. I could fear that panther,

or First Nation apparitions, but really, whatever excuses I have for you,
I don't climb down that bank and walk the creek bed at sunrise

because I'm too content. I'm cozy here. The slope is steep, ticks and
chiggers, hang on every branch and grass blade. Nature is a mixed bag for
me,

even on a morning as beautiful as this, wild iris tickling each other beside
the rocks, and the daylight urgent and promising as a kiss. My preference, if
I confess,

is for ease. At my desk, doing no more than this, imagining their wounded
feet and faces, the human and coyote, the mountain lion, the primrose and
daisy, the oak.

Paulette Guerin

Ginkgo
Ginkgo biloba

Paulette Guerin

I studied creative writing at Louisiana State University, the stomping grounds of the New Critics and where I learned to trust the image. I earned an MA in English and American literature from the University of Central Arkansas and then taught courses in world literature, poetry, fiction, and drama. After completing an MFA in poetry writing from the University of Florida, I worked as a freelance manuscript editor for a range of scholarly and creative works. I now teach writing, literature, and film at Harding University.

My chapbook, *Polishing Silver* (2011), was a finalist for Finishing Line Press's annual chapbook competition, and my debut poetry collection *Wading Through Lethe* was published by FutureCycle Press in 2022. My poetry has appeared in *Best New Poets*, *2 River View*, *epiphany*, *Contemporary Verse 2*, and others. Please visit pauletteguerin.com for more details.

I spent much of my early life living in Little Rock in a small condo, accustomed to the swish of cars and shrill sirens, hot asphalt, and the glare of sun on metal. Two hours away, in the Ozarks, my grandmother, a schoolteacher, lived in a log cabin miles from anywhere and anyone. She loved Robert Frost, wrote poetry, and lived close to the land.

My first memory of the Ozarks: I'm five years old going "to the mountains" for a week-long stay at Grandma's. Although I brought bags of toys, afraid I would run out of things to do, I didn't play with any of them—my days were full of other things: digging in the dirt pile, walking to the pond, collecting hickory nuts, harvesting vegetables from the garden, and feeding the chickens.

Although I was used to a flurry of kids in our city neighborhood, I found many more companions in this remote, isolated patch of land—the collies, the beagle flopped on her back for a belly pat, the chickens (particularly the slow and friendly Mrs. Featherfoot), and deer darting across the dirt road. Night was punctuated by the loud croaks of bullfrogs, deafening cicada song, and coyote howls. It was the first time I felt awe in the sense of both amazement and fear. In the city, my knowledge of flora and fauna included pine trees, grass, holly bushes, and ants, and most of my roaming was in a car or heavily supervised. At Grandma's, the world offered a thousand sensory experiences at once and the freedom to explore them— pink dogwoods, a rescued one-winged owl clicking its beak, the sweet smell of corn feed and the sound of kernels sliding against the rusted coffee can, the gift of fresh air, and the many shades of green in the woods.

When I was almost ten, my family moved to the Ozarks to be closer to my grandmother. We lived near Greers Ferry Lake in an area not nearly as wild but with its own beauty and magic. Growing up in both the city and the country gave me a dual citizenship and the ability to see each place at a distance. Because of the early visits to my grandmother's, my experience of nature became inextricably linked to the Ozarks. Then, after years of living in the mountains, and especially after leaving, I learned how the land becomes part of one's identity. For better or worse, humans have a relationship with their surroundings, and the Ozarks are a rich and boundless place to live. They taught me the healing power of nature, our dependence on it, and our inability to truly control it. The wildness of nature reminds me of my own impermanence and that nothing is guaranteed. But it also gives me a reverence for life and an opportunity to be fully present to the minutia as well as the larger unfolding.

The Ozarks are their own world, a world I carry with me—a love of land and preservation that my grandmother taught me and that I seek to pass on. Poetry is one way I can access the past and make meaning, since it offers a way to condense experience. Writing poetry, which for me is also a process of discovery, makes the difficult parts of life easier to bear by naming them, and it brings the beautiful into focus.

Roots

The condos stood like dominoes.
Without a line for sky and land to meet,
even sunny days had long shadows.
Mother's tulips went missing,
and then our home looked like every other,
the same sad squares for windows.

One day we left. I learned the way sunlight
can fill a field of hay and rain pound
a tin roof through the night.
Amid baying coyotes and bullfrog moans, I found
a pink dogwood deep in the shadowed canopy,
its rare color drawn from the ground.

Visit

When the rooster roused us, the sun
was already splashing through the blinds.
Hens pecked chiggers in the tick-filled yard,
and guineas flocked to the fir tree.

The daddy longlegs crowded
beneath the awning, each with its beady body
and slink-walk. Grandma picked up one
and asked it which way the cows had gone.

One of the legs pointed toward the pasture,
so we began asking them other questions:
where to find treasure, which way home,
where our parents were.

First Communion

The night before, Grandma made my pallet
on the couch with faded blue flowers.

Across the room, the iron-barrel stove loomed.
We learned not to touch it.

At midnight I woke. I'd never heard rain on a tin roof
and was sure what Revelation promised was true—

dark horses had come. In church we'd learned
about the wise and foolish virgins with their oil.

I had not confessed my sins. Everyone else slept—
or were they gone? Then the rain let up.

The dark turned dim. I chipped the polish
from my nails, ashamed they were not bare.

In the Ozarks

The swollen goat, too sore to feed, kicks back
her hungry kid. A whippoorwill cuts through
the cold as acorns fall into wet leaves.
Coyotes pluck a mallard from its pack,
howling until the moon fades into blue
and daylight strains the stars out of its sieve.

Beads of sleet

stacked themselves along the woodpile, filling
every crevice between logs. I could measure the depth

there, how much had fallen in how much time.
No one had promised snow, but we weren't expecting ice.

All the city salt had been poured out for last week's scare,
or elsewhere. It didn't matter. We were happy

by the fire, happy not to be in school. We couldn't build
a snowman, or stumble into fallen angels

on the ground. Without sun, the woods darkened
into a fairy tale. We plucked the rare, gray pearl.

Mountain Air

Mornings, the air filtered through window screens,
heavy with the moisture

that waked the grass. In winter,
the air was clean and crisp; in drought, alive

with dust and pine. The smell descending
with dusk told us the time,

that our minutes were being swallowed
into the blue glow along the horizon,

where, in summer, we stayed under the stars,
sky blacker than coffee or tar.

Mercy

An early morning storm closes
around us like a fist, shallow light
wrung out in little pools.

Mold smudges darken on the house;
trees along the fence-line
twinge black. Wearing his overalls,

Grandpa would have said, *It's tornado weather*,
but the air isn't yet the color
of a nearly-healed bruise—green

with yellow glow. It's only water
clouding the distance, no heaven-earth
entanglements. A simple fall.

Night Out at Cadron Creek Catfish House,
Choctaw, Arkansas

The black truck rocks
in every washed-out pothole,

the ruts dug deep on the homestretch
where last autumn's flood

filled the ditches with mud. In the headlights,
a luna moth's green eyes flutter.

Then, the quick flit of bat sounds out its prey
with every flapped wing.

Owl

After Grandma hit the owl with her truck,
a vet removed the dangling wing.

She raised rats for him to hunt
in the seven-foot cage. Sometimes dinner

was a slab of cold, raw meat.
We watched him click his beak,

lids slide over glassy eyes.
Autumn nights I prayed

into the darkness of shivering leaves,
cricket-song, and flightless cries.

One summer

we picked wild blackberries by lanterns
when dusk fell, when it was almost cool

enough to breathe, when the mosquitoes
found us by our exhale. The plump berries

that slipped through my fingers
and fell into darkness I didn't dare reach for,

leaving them as an offering to the ground.
I left with the thorns' kisses scrawled

into my arms, mosquito bites in tender
places, berry blood on my lips.

Summer, Greers Ferry Lake

Like graduating seniors, the cicadas emerged
after seventeen years in the ground,
starved and full of lust. I waited
for one boy's annual return,
on vacation at our lake cupped in the Ozarks.
The trees hadn't been fully painted in,
needing a hard rain and a few hot days
to brush the landscape fat and green.

The dry creek-bed moved with mating,
their song swarming us to silence. At the end
of August, the sun resigned, the water turned cold.
I woke from our dream. Shells littered
the ground like candy wrappers,
then vanished beneath the leaves.

The Far Side of the Mountain

Beneath the murk lay my fishing hat, somewhere
in the marina his boat. I imagine the lake
as it once was: two low-lying towns, their graveyards,
the dead's peace disturbed for higher ground.

Mother never let us swim to the buoys,
so I drove backroads to the cliffs,
dove into a deeper green. Sugarloaf Mountain loomed,

the lone god of the lake. Now I see it
from the other side, a distant, pitiful shade.
I wonder if Eurydice, once back in Hades,
still hummed some song she'd heard Orpheus play.

Signs

Every year the maple at the top of the hill
cried the brightest yellow,
and if you blinked you missed it—
the hill sloped so steeply, a roller coaster
racing into a sharp curve. The tree, a cautionary
sign to all recklessly fast teenage drivers
of the peak and plunge. No place to stop, pull off
to admire the golden hue, growing more golden
against gray skies, like all moments of beauty:
doomed to brevity, never quite real,
fashioned later and for years afterward.

Childhood

A crepe myrtle dangles
over the swimming hole:
brief, pink waves.

Diminuendo

We left the upright, one side propped
with *As I Lay Dying*, decaled roses peeling,
the black varnish buckled after years
of playing *Sonata No. 8 in C Minor*. A train rolled by,
the strings humming in its wake.

We packed the row of photographs
above the missing ivory. I picked up
Mother's cricket cage, the only thing
for which she'd ever paid full price.

Yellow leaves shimmied to the ground. A new moon
kept the sky dark, the stars too weak.
I almost left the key in the birdfeeder tray.

Ginkgo

Through rain-thrash
and wind-sear,
the stems cling
to each limb.

After other trees
have metamorphosed
green to gold,
red to brown,
stems rattle in the dawn.

The ginkgo waits
then lets go.
Brief burst
of yellow.

Emily Dickinson Floats the Buffalo River

She regrets wearing white,
        the edge of her dress muddied.
        Down she drifts—
catching a whiff of charred food
        and a faint Skynyrd riff,

past purple flowers she deems gentians.
            The canoe paddle
        stirs the tawny fish. She calls them cod,
the water clear
            down to the riverbed's
        algaed stones.
Just beyond the shadow of a cliff,
            the rapids come.
        She cannot stop

thinking of the river's nonchalance—
            its only thought, resistance;
        —its only love,
change. Evening light
                shifts the tableau—
        viridian and burnt ocher
blend to muted indigo.

        Just when she seems at home,
Dickinson pens a postcard—
        "How can I stand
    this tighter Breathing,
        this Zero
            at the bone?"

Bluest

I fill the feeder full and wait.

One morning a bunting appears—
the color I've always wanted
blue to be.

A blue that is its own music,
its own trill.
A Hello! blue, a wake-up-

it's-midday blue,
a blue that asks
what have you done

with your life?

Cabin in the Ozarks

We take my daughter there,
contactless check-in, a safe vacation
in the mountains. She's never seen wall-to-wall wood,
each knot a star in the ceiling.

Three years old, she's afraid to sleep alone,
so when the fireflies appear outside the window,
I tell her they bring good dreams;
they color the night gold.

She sleeps better here than back home,
wakes with the dawn. I find her at the French door
peering into the valley: two wild turkeys
strutting in the glow of five-thirty.

When they disappear, we go to look for them.
She rides piggyback while I dance around
poison ivy. At the bottom of the hill, the clearing
isn't all that clear. More underbrush, more green,

nothing to explore. I wash our clothes, check for ticks.
We complete a puzzle of fish. Her father builds a fire
for her first s'mores. We sit on simple wooden chairs
purified by smoke.

End of Autumn

Sometimes a storm comes when autumn is at its best.
The wind, a bull charging beneath the treetops, slings color

with every trunk it rams. There should be a name
for the wind that picks off every red leaf, that stuns

the yellows and orange to brown, that drinks the purple,
dark as wine, that wrestles everything to the ground;

that takes the trees' heavy load, hisses at any limbs it misses
until they give up their tiny ghosts.

We take bets on which November day will be the last.

Weaving

Outside, muscadine vines soaked in the clawfoot tub
like tangled strands of hair.

After two days, Grandma showed us how to weave them
over and under the wire stars.

Lined along the porch, our crude baskets leached dry
while maples bellowed orange.

This year, as the autumn leaves barely speak,
I count the years she's been gone.

Parasite

We watched as the ruby-throats flocked
to the trumpet creeper's red flowers.
September's fever had broken; the hummers
were headed south. We drained
the plastic kiddie pool, algae-slick,
unfurled the cedar chest's sweaters.
Leaves hissed and fluttered umber;
eggplant and squash, fresh-picked,
colored our meals. Mist rose in wisps
with a late sun. When frost wilted the vine,
the redbud lay beneath, raptured,
its heart-shaped leaves turning gold to rust.
A snapped limb dangled, its spine
wet with rot, long dead.

Old Trees

We drove North on potholed highways,
down into gullies and over slow-moving creeks.
When we reached the city limits,
we lost, for a moment, where we were.

The last ice storm had picked off the oldest trees,
the sound of splitting limbs haunting
the town for days. We passed a sign for firewood,
then pulled over to walk among what remained.

Mountains were stacked in weakening shades of blue,
the furthest line as light as sky.
I stopped to count the rings, the scent
of wood still sweet.

Winter Hike

The snow fell lightly that year, feather down.
The sleet had finally found another town.
My eyes were set on someone's summer home
embedded in the bluff. I went alone

across the snow's erasures, colder air
the further up I climbed. No other there,
the woods grew quiet in the early dark.
I found the wooden stairs up to the deck.

The scene itself a simple Rorschach: white—
the trunks and limbs, a splattering of ink.
No photo would reveal the staggered hills,
ecstatic air, all nature on the brink.

Goodbye

I take my daughter to the carriage house
before the land is sold. She's never seen it,
and may be too young to remember even this visit.

Still we rock along the smooth stones
of the canopied drive. The grapevines have dried,
after years of us trying to wrestle their sweetness into wine.

She must see the land her great-great-grandmother bought,
the tiny woman who was always making plans,
who said the farm would save us when the world ended.

She prophesied the floods would come,
the sea level rise and set its shore along the Ozarks.
God had shown her famine years ahead.

She bought goats and a wood chopper,
baled hay until she was 93. She was deaf in one ear
since girlhood, after a spider crawled in and bit.

She could hear only herself speak;
enough to preach to the rest of us who had fallen
away from church, we who worked for nothing

in cities, too much a part of this world.
My daughter never knew her. She poses
beside the surprise lilies, gone tomorrow.

John J. Han

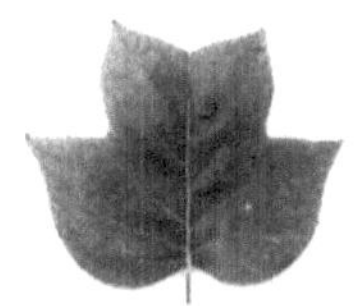

Yellow Poplar
Liriodendron tulipifera

John J. Han

I am a professor of English and creative writing and chair of the humanities division at Missouri Baptist University in St. Louis. This is my twenty-fourth year of teaching as a full-time faculty member and my fifteenth year serving as an administrator at MBU. After attending elementary and middle schools in the South Korean countryside, I began to pursue my education in two big cities, Gwangju and Seoul. After earning my BA in English language and literature and my MEd in English from Kookmin and Yonsei Universities in Seoul, respectively, I earned an MA in English from Kansas State University and a PhD in English from the University of Nebraska-Lincoln. My doctoral dissertation was on T. S. Eliot and Flannery O'Connor. My academic interests include Flannery O'Connor, John Steinbeck, Ozarks authors, psychology and literature, popular literature, haiku poetics, and Asian poetry.

I am the author, editor, co-editor, or translator of 30 books, including *Wise Blood: A Re-Consideration* (Rodopi, 2011), *The Final Crossing: Death and Dying in Literature* (Peter Lang, 2015) and *Worlds Gone Awry: Essays on Dystopian Fiction* (McFarland, 2018). More than 2,000 of my poems have appeared in periodicals and anthologies worldwide, including *Cave Region Review* (featured poet for 2012), *Chrysanthemum*, *Elder Mountain*, *Failed Haiku*, *Frogpond*, *Kansas English*, *The Laurel Review*, *Modern Haiku*, *Simply Haiku* (chosen as the world's sixth-finest English-language haiku poet for 2011), *Steinbeck Studies*, *Valley Voices* (Pushcart-nominated), *Wales Haiku Journal*, and *World Haiku Review*. Finally, I served as the editor of the 2022 Haiku Society of America members' anthology.

Poets write about what they love. Some poets are keen on sociopolitical issues, others are philosophically oriented, and still others turn to nature for inspiration. I am not an activist of any kind, and I do not use poetry as a form of philosophical discourse. My poetry is nature-based because I love the natural world more than anything. I grew up in nature, learned to appreciate it, and have found consolation in it. The love of nature can be acquired, but it is ingrained in the psyche of those who grow up amid natural surroundings.

My life began in 1956—three years after the end of the Korean War—along the southwestern coastline of the Korean Peninsula. I grew up among peasants who grew rice and barley in the fields across the Yellow Sea from mainland China. Living far from the modern world, I had ample opportunities to observe the seasonal changes in and around my village: wildflowers sprouting on the spring banks, the summer raindrops falling on the irrigation canal, the ripe rice making waves in an autumn wind, and the snow-covered fields in wintertime. Having grown up as a country boy, I have never felt comfortable in a big city.

After deciding to come to the United States for graduate studies, I chose the Great Plains as my destination. Living in Manhattan, Kansas, for three years, and then living in Lincoln, Nebraska, for eight years were unforgettable experiences. Living close to wheat fields, corn fields, and hog farms, I almost felt like I had come back home. After moving to St. Louis, I have developed an attraction to the Ozarks, a region of hills and valleys that does not look as intimidating as the Rockies. Not surprisingly, many of my poetic images come from my native village, the Great Plains, and the Ozarks.

An increasing number of my new poems deal with death and dying as related to nature. Now, in my mid-sixties, nature does not merely provide pleasant scenes. The natural world is still dear to my heart, but it has also become a place I shall return to once my time is up. My ashes shall become part of the soil—as did those of numerous people before my time. Death used to prompt sadness, but not anymore. For me, it means cessation from strife and an eternal rest in nature, which is a comforting thought.

Where Does the Ozarks Begin?

(A haibun)

Some maps of the Ozarks exclude St. Louis County, Missouri. As a long-time resident of the County, however, I think that Lone Elk Park and Castlewood State Park—located within the County, only a few miles away from my neighborhood—should be considered part of the Ozarks. The former has hills and hollers, and the latter has hills, bluffs, and the Meramec River. My county doesn't have "mountain people" but seems to have plenty of wannabe mountaineers who love to hunt and fish. So, my theory is that the northeastern territory of the Ozarks begins in the southwestern corner of St. Louis County.

> troubled world
> signing up for
> mandolin lessons

The Sunny Spot

(A haibun)

On the hiking trail along the Meramec River in St. Louis County, Missouri, there is a new wooden bench. It bears the Chinese and English name of a man who died in his mid-fifties. I don't know how he died, but the bench takes the best spot along the trail. It faces west, viewing the river flowing from mid-Missouri and miles of rolling hills. I often sit on the bench, wondering what brought the man to the United States and what he thought about life on his deathbed.

> Amida Buddha's call
> fallen leaves drift
> westward

Living Under the Shadow of Death

(A haibun)

In East Asia, some older adults used to buy coffins and place them in their bedrooms. The presence of a coffin gave them the comfort of knowing where they would lie after their passing. Medieval monks kept a human skeleton on their desks as a reminder of the ephemeral nature of life. In the current age of medical breakthroughs, living with a coffin or a human skeleton may seem morbid. However, before the rise of modern medicine, death was not something of a distant future. At the turn of the twentieth century, the average lifespan for Americans was 49. In medieval Europe, life expectancy at birth was 33, and in the Roman Empire, it was a mere 25 years. Life is precious, yet it would be unwise to cling to it. Living life to the fullest yet going with the flow of nature—this seems to be the secret to happiness many sages in the world have discovered.

> glowing
> for a month or two
> fireflies

Four Seasons: Tanka

spring breeze
in the backyard
a cat chases
a dog that chases
a rabbit

midsummer
cicada sounds
on and
on and
on

late-autumn crickets
some peppy
others flabby
still others
doleful

midwinter
awake at night
all of a sudden
remembering
a long-lost name

Snapshots of Summer: Haiku

summer breeze
a baby turtle peeks
out of its shell

corn tassels
flaxen hair caressed
by the wind

Father's Day
teaching my puppy
how to swim

cicadas
debating whether
they sing or scream

the lover cat
heedless of the spread
of COVID-19

summer night
the roar of baseball fans
on a cul-de-sac

Autumn Haiku

serene autumn
the neighbor's cat
mid-musing

autumn wind
letting it
go

fallen leaves
in place until
wind blows

autumn in the Ozarks
beyond the hills
blue calmness

the tall oak
midway a squirrel decides
to climb down

Autumn in the Ozarks: Haiku

scenic route
the shimmering of red
yellow orange

October drive
the crack crack crack
of acorns

flipping through radio stations-
country, country, country,
God, country

a yellow butterfly
gliding in the breeze
I spread my arms

out for red leaves . . .
getting distracted by
a red dragonfly

autumn breeze
haystacks don't budge
tall grass sways

November sun
a scampering squirrel
and its shadow

Deepening Autumn

(Fibonacci)

a ripe persimmon fruit perches
on the Ozarks hill
tinted with
flames of
the
sun

cold
dew
touching
my bare feet
an empty bird's nest
autumn deepens as days shorten

An Autumn Evening

(A cento)

Autumn—the sea and the fields, one green.
Any greenness is deeper than anyone knows.
The yellow pears hang in the lake.
Season of mists and mellow fruitfulness!
Calligraphy of geese against the sky—the moon seals it.
Evening cicada—a last nearby song to autumn.
Cowbells sound in the dusk from winter pastures.
Sleep seems a goodly thing in autumn.

Sources:
1.   Basho's haiku
2.   Richard Wilbur, "The Beautiful Changes"
3.   David Lehman, "Autumn Evening"
4.   John Keats, "To Autumn"
5.   Buson's haiku
6.   Issa's haiku
7.   W. S. Merwin, "Autumn Evening"
8.   Dante Gabriel Rossetti, "Autumn Song"

Autumn Squirrels: Haiku

autumn harmony
a yellow butterfly
on a yellow mum

languor in the air
the slow movement
of a squirrel

autumn weariness
a squirrel struggles
over the fence

reaped fields
a squirrel eating
and eating

night chill
a squirrel's long pause
on fading grass

A Nightly Encounter

(A haibun)

Growing up in the Korean rice fields was neither pastoral nor lyrical. Hills and mountains at the end of the fields blocked my view of a more glamorous world—cities of neon signs, cars, movie theaters, pretty girls. Upon finishing rural middle school, I left home to attend a high school in the provincial capital. Three years later, I moved to Seoul—a city of ten million people—for a college education. My parents did not know I was more interested in the charm of urban life than in my education.

As imagined, Seoul was lovely—high-rise buildings cast shadows over the busy streets, there were numerous palatial gardens to visit, girls sounded more cultured than those in the countryside. Although Seoul soon revealed itself as a place of unkindness, I continued to live there for fifteen years, pursuing higher education, launching my lifelong career, and starting my own family.

When I turned thirty, I decided that it was time for a change—for a big change. After selling our house, my family and I moved to Eastern Kansas for my master's degree at a state university in the Flint Hills. In September of the first semester, I studied until after midnight. Then, stepping out of my room for fresh air, I rediscovered what I had lost since my childhood—a clear, expansive sky.

    crickets chirping
    the night sky spills
    stars

Smitten with the Hills

(A haibun)

As a "flatlander," I discovered the beauty of the Ozarks nearly ten years ago while driving in northern Arkansas and southern Missouri. The radio was playing Dolly Parton's twangy song about lost love, and the hills along the winding road were covered with glittery fall leaves. Later, I discovered the same beauty while reading Harold Bell Wright's novel *The Shepherd of the Hills* (1907), in which the author praises the region's forest-clad hills and valleys. The Ozark Plateau has become my newest passion, and I deem myself as a suburbanite who is a hillbilly—a ridge runner—at heart.

> riding a bike
> in my native village
> autumn dream

Departing Autumn

(A haibun)

The signs are everywhere. A barbecue grill sitting alone in the back yard.
An empty bird's nest up the tree. Leaves turning red, orange, and yellow.
Cold dewdrops touching unwary feet. Days shorten.

> harvested fields
> the combine disappears
> into the sun

Winter Haiku

cold drizzle
the foggy glow
of the moon

winter wind
a homeless man adds leaves
to his clothing

fallen leaves
a feral child befriends
a feral cat

vagrant's death
the tail of a stray cat
leaving my porch

yuletide
hanging socks again
except our dog's

Sights and Sounds of Winter: Haiku

warm winter
a puppy drags
his master

December sunlight
both the squirrel and
its shadow

warm winter sun
snow in the north yard
almost melts

cold wave
snow on snow that has
yet to melt

thickening ice
one more layer of
clothing

north wind
a distant memory of
cicadas

southward wind
stranded in the land
wild geese deserted

polar vortex
the freezing sound of
a pine grove

Arctic currents
passing through
an oak grove

deep freeze
my dog can't find his
favorite spot

Arkansas: Travel Haiku

slow traffic
even without
a patrol car

country road
sunlight spills over
Indian pink

gentle wind
gentle shaking
of jonquils

hill after hill
after hill after hill
after hill after . . .

squirrels . . .
they look the same as
Missouri squirrels

Winter Mountain: Haiku

first snow . . .
all viewers have left except
the moon and me

running around
with friends in deep snow . . .
squirrels

surprising each other
on a deserted trail . . .
a deer and I

floating ice . . .
migrating bald eagles
on board

snowy tree . . .
a sudden flutter
of a cardinal

snowy trail . . .
shoe prints of
different patterns

frosty night
clouds scrambling
this way and that

frozen waterfall . . .
wild geese glide over
the empty hill

sudden splashes
from the mountain lake . . .
waterfowl

snowflakes . . .
serene owl with
eyes closed

Snapshots of Winter: Haiku

all that remains
this December night
the memory of crickets

winter encounter
a deer stands
frozen

winter woods
snow falls from branch
to branch

winter river
a pile of snow
on a deserted boat

winter wind
continuing our talk
on death and dying

Ozark Beauty: Haiku

spring rain
the overflow of
a birdbath

crystal stream
the contours of
a fiddle sound

woodland pond
the reflection of
a flitting sparrow

summer night
rediscovering the stars
from childhood

harvested fields
lengthening shadows
of haystacks

autumn hills
maple leaves dripping
red, red, red

October rain
a maple leaf clinging
to the window

evening trail
a squirrel's crossing followed
by a falling leaf

autumn twilight
a house wren alighting
on a cattail

dusk over hills
missing an old friend who
didn't live to see this

Cat Haiku

coming of spring
my first guest at the door
a stray cat

spring inspection
a neighbor's cat patrols
my backyard

morning sunlight
the long stretch of
a cat's shadow

closing the garage door
a cat's head up, down, up,
down, down

midday sun
with eyes closed,
a cat licks his paws

twilight
a cat's eyes
glow red

time for bed—
the departing cat leaves
no sound

reading Ginsberg's "Howl"
the neighbor's living room
emits a howl

Spring 2020: Haiku

balmy day
a breeze reveals
her petticoat

spring sunlight
a baby woodpecker peeks
out of a tree hole

spring appetite
nectar drips from
a hummingbird bill

cleaning nonstop
an expecting woodpecker
can't do enough

dad on the lookout
mom robin feeds
their young

pandemic
receiving ashes
with face masks on

pandemic
robins linger longer
on the street

virus lockdown
peering out at
an ice cream truck

Squirrels Gone Wild

(A pantoum poem)

It's spring break.
Squirrels gone wild in my ceiling.
At night, they chase each other, keeping me wide awake.
We cohabit—me in my bed, the critters in the ceiling.

Squirrels gone wild in my ceiling.
They never ever sleep.
We cohabit—me in my bed, the critters in the ceiling.
Their rowdy party forces me not to sleep.

They never ever sleep.
Their clatter gives me the chills.
Their rowdy party forces me not to sleep.
I need strong sleeping pills.

Their clatter gives me the chills.
My mind needs a break.
I need strong sleeping pills.
It's spring break.

Spring Rain

(Fibonacci)

rain
rain
all through
the spring night…
I lie awake, praying
my dogwood blossoms stay intact

*

rain
and
thunder . . .
dozens of
magnolia petals
scattered over the spring garden

*

young
birds
don't chirp
this morning . . .
from under a bush
they view a new thing: a cloudburst

The Lake of the Ozarks

(A sedōka)

a Magic Dragon
with a serpentine coastline
longer than California's
its head faces east
its horn reaches Gravois Mills
its tail touches Niangua

Springtime Japanese Garden

(Double Fibonacci)

A
blue
sky is
mirrored in
the pond, where tiny
ripples shake the reflection. Pink
and white, lotus flowers float on
the water's surface.
Cherry trees
erupt
in
pink.

Spring Haiku

clifftop in springtime
a bluebell bends
toward the sea

coming of spring
a gosling tests
the waters

only because
the in-laws are coming
spring cleaning

spring meadow
the goat's long leap
through tulips

spring allergies
the sneeze keeps people
six feet away

spring wind
two robins on
an undulating branch

April
my dog pees on the last
of the snowman

On a Spring Morning

(A haibun)

It is spring—the season of birth and renewal. Birds compete in chirping and pick up dried leaves to build nests. As snow melts, clear water dangles from maple branches. Squirrels jump, rabbits run in the yard. This bright Saturday morning, I am sitting at a funeral—a funeral of a teenage girl who ended her life.

> gray morning
> early buds nipped
> by frost

Phillip Howerton

Blackjack Oak
Quercus marilandica

Photo by Sarita Rivera

Phillip Howerton

I was brought up on a small dairy farm in southern Dallas County, Missouri, about three miles from where my ancestors settled in the 1830s. After spending several years as a milk truck driver, beef farmer, and production worker, I earned degrees in English, history, and education from Drury University and a doctorate in American literature and rhetoric and composition from University of Missouri-Columbia.

I am a professor of English, co-founder and co-editor of *Cave Region Review*, and general editor of *Elder Mountain: A Journal of Ozarks Studies*, and my poetry has appeared in numerous literary journals. My poetry collection, *The History of Tree Roots*, was published by Golden Antelope Press in 2015, and the University of Arkansas Press released my anthology, *The Literature of the Ozarks*, in 2019. I am currently completing a collection of poems, essays, and photographs entitled *Gods of Four Mile Creek*.

As a kid on a small, work intensive, old-fashioned farm, I met the natural world face to face and hand to hand most every day. Our livelihood depended on the health and behavior of the natural world, and nature was omnipresent: the wind in the trees, the rattle or roar of the wet-weather creek, the heat of the fields, the storms, the mud on my boots, the taste of wild onions in our raw milk at breakfast. Every chore, every meal, and most every moment of day and night was inseparable from nature.

One daily chore illustrates this absolute connection. We milked a small herd of Holsteins, and the first task every morning, an hour or two before dawn, was to bring the cows to the barn. This had to be done every day regardless of weather, regardless of lightning storms, flooded creeks, sub-zero weather, or a foot of fresh snow. Few things can make a youngster more aware of the natural world than a dark daily morning trek through fields, across a creek, into woods by only the light of the stars or moon—or no stars and moon. Nature was ever present in my past, so it is always there when I engage memories. It is as much a part of my poetry as the alphabet.

Seldom do I give myself the task of writing a nature poem, but I rarely write a poem without nature. Among my selections included here, only "Rain Crow" is the result of such self-assignment. In this poem, I chose to use the folklore of rain crows predicting rain to comment upon climate change. Nature usually finds its way into my writing without me forcing it in. For example, most every spring, sometimes as early as late February, I see Small Bluets on the south side of a hill or ditch, which immediately reminds me of digging clumps of these tiny fellows for my mother. She would put them in an upturned jar lid and place them in her kitchen window above the sink. I didn't go in search of this little poem; it found me long ago and had been sitting on the windowsill of my mind, waiting for me to notice.

Another example of such finding is "While Cleaning the Shed," which took almost fifty years to circle to my hands. I have often recalled that long-ago summer when my dad took time from the summer fields to treat my brother and me to nights on the Niangua River. I had often been tempted to write about that summer, but childhood experiences are a minefield of sentimentality and are rarely of interest to anyone other than the owner. Then, while cleaning a shed after my father's death, I found a boat oar my older brother had made that summer, and with it came a universal theme.

Sometimes nature perches on the lines of a poem in such an obvious fashion that we cannot see that the poem is not about nature. Perhaps it's an overstatement to say that a poem should never be about what it first appears to be about, but it must give more than what is immediately seen. Nature can always be concrete—sometimes a snake is simply a snake—but more often, nature serves as a multi-blossoming metaphor, and the possum is no longer a possum, the whippoorwill is no longer a whippoorwill, and the broken wild cherry trees become those elderly, grief-tortured farmers who once stood on the horizons of my rural childhood.

Small Bluets

Hedyotis crassifloia

We find them blinking new-born
eyes in March long before we
have thought to dream
of flowers. The closer we
look, the tinier they become
until each of their four
pointed petals is smaller
than a vole's nose. We
spade up a handful of soil
containing a blue colony
and place them in a jar lid
on the windowsill
above the kitchen sink
from where they,
a native and wild bonsai,
pull the rest of life
into the correct proportions.

Barn Removal

The barn swallows return again
by instinct, following a homing device
to this place where a barn stood
for more than a century.
Torn down during winter,
only its foundation remains,
ruins beyond the birds' reckoning,
and they dive and circle,
almost losing grace to confusion,
and then they alight on a power wire
and tap their instrument panels.

Mayapple

Podophyllum peltatum

> *Despite its name, the plant blooms in March
> in the Ozarks (farther north it blooms in
> May); furthermore, it is not an apple but
> a member of the barberry family.*
> Richard Rhodes
> *The Ozarks*

Perhaps the locals
got it wrong,
but the Mayapple
was known
not for beauty,
but for use,
not for bloom,
but for fruit.
Blossoming in March,
it bears in May
that which
only those who
have gathered it
in a past
of need and delight
and memory
can now know;
and when it ripened,
sweet and butter yellow,
so early after winter,
and long before melons
or blackberries,
it was an apple.

Opossum

It comes at night to pilfer
my back lawn
for a potato peel or heel
of tomato or for corn
wasted by red squirrels.
There is a primitive ugliness
about its busy nose,
tatty ears, reptilian tail,
and gray, ratty fur.
An obstinate beggar,
the dogs ignore it now
as I rattle the doorknob
to send it scurrying
back to darkness,
leaving only a footprint,
like a small, deformed hand,
in the damp earth.

Mayflies in the Foyer of a Nursing Home

Having fulfilled their duty to the species,
they arrive in this artificial world,
this sterile fluorescence,
where, on four fragile lacy wings
they bump against concrete walls,
flutter in lemon-scented confusion,
until they sit still,
drawn into themselves, comatose.
We feel a slight embarrassment in their presence
and cannot imagine their former lives—
hatching from eggs laid in water,
gulping life through gills,
feeding upon water plants—
but they have slipped those skins
to become *subimago*, sub-adults
without mouth or stomach,
bereft of voice and appetite.
Entomologists believe them the only insects,
perhaps the only living beings,
to undergo this stage of metamorphosis.

On a Bluff Overlooking the Buffalo National River

Few monuments commemorate
those who lost home
to treaty, poverty, or law—
but they would refuse
any memorial offered
by those who take
and do not understand the loss,
so perhaps this ancient cedar
standing in its crucible
of stone, wind, and sky
high above the river
is the most fitting marker
as it spins ring
upon ring of thin years
around its knotted heart.

Whippoorwill

Folklorists report that it was believed
to be the call of death, but we never
held such superstitions and welcomed it
when it came to call at dusk.
Beginning its chant in the shadows
of woods, it would flutter closer
to continue its vigil in the path
leading from the back porch to the barn,
and I would lie awake and watch
shadows of the walnut leaves
on the wall and listen to the slow
breath of my sleeping brother
and to my parents talking each other
to sleep, and then I would drift off
wrapped in the belief that it would be forever
before any of that life would pass away.

Bloodroot
Sanguinaria canadensis

It prefers the moist, lower slopes
of rocky, wooded hillsides;
suspicious and tight-lipped,
it offers a single blossom
for only one day,
white and daisy-like,
and then remains a single leaf
wedged low out of earth,
hiding its joy among ground cover,
but throbbing from root tip
to leaf tip with blood
drawn from the thin soil
to which it clings.

The Redbuds

O, let me not be mad, not mad, sweet heaven!
King Lear

Surely we tolerate and cultivate them
for more than their brief purple beauty,
for they fade into shade of taller trees
and shadows of their heavy heart-like leaves,
where they spend the remainder of time
harming themselves, twisting and torturing
their trunks, ranging limbs out in impossible
angles as though begging wind and ice
to break them, and they grow mad and gray,
shed shingles of thinning bark, go hollow,
and we find them in early spring
where they have thrown themselves prone,
exhausted and spent in their despair,
and we prop them up with a cinder block
or cord wood as they remind us of what we
must not allow ourselves to do or be.

The History of Tree Roots

My ancestors settled on these banks
perhaps by accident, delivered here
by high winds or high water,
and they put down roots so deep
that they became the identity of this place—
but few locals now know the name
of this stream, and its seasonal rise
wears away the course of the past;
yet I remain, misshapen by my seeking
of fissures, by my grasping of stones,
becoming the contours of resistance,
the contortions of my resilience,
holding in place what little remains
of a soil that once held me secure.

Gods of Four Mile Creek

They sometimes tried to mimic Greek cousins
but could manage only poorest of plays,
killing luckless crawdads and tadpoles
by withholding waters, and when raging
at full froth, they would wash away a water gate
or drown a hay bale loitering in a low field.
They were often absent for months;
free of them, the creek would grow calm,
and water striders and sycamore leaves
would glide the surface, or, if in winter,
water gurgled beneath a shell of arched ice
in shallows or laid silent in frozen eddies.

But they always returned to continue
seasonal antics of fall and rise, pushing
gravel into the bottom pastures, piling
trash in young bent willows, whispering
to me in morning darkness, and threatening
my footing as I waded to fetch milk cows.
Unloving, yet certain of our love,
they were not jealous, demanded no proof
of faith; they knew we were like the fishes
that fought their way upstream each spring
returning to pools that would soon dry away.
In riffles we could hear their laughter,
for they knew we would always return,
and they believed they had nothing to give.

Rain Crow

My ancestors believed
they knew when
rains would come
and spent hours talking
in their doorways
about the weather,
filling woods
with hoots and coos
of divination, but
that skill is now
dismissed as folklore
and the sky grows ever
more unpredictable,
so now no one listens to
or knows how to interpret
my cries of bewildered error.

On Her Blindness

I don't remember being aware at age four
that Mother was losing her eyesight;
my attention was captured by the grasshopper
I held prisoner in a Mason jar who kept eyes
upon escape when I inserted fresh grass;
by the bubble-eyed tadpoles I had scooped
from the creek and placed in a fish bowl;
and by how strange my name sounded when I
said it aloud with eyes closed; but I
sometimes cried on moonless nights
when darkness consumed my room.
She would come to my side and whisper,
"Don't be afraid. There's no reason to fear
the dark," but I would not be comforted.

While Cleaning the Shed

Behind clutter, leaning against the back wall,
a boat oar, one of a pair older brother shaped
from an oak board more than fifty years ago.
For two weeks that summer dad took us
early from hay fields to night fish the river,
nights of floating under and on a stream of stars,
tying limb lines, listening to the countless choir
of minute mouths, peering into silent depths,
and then falling asleep by lantern light. The boat
rotted away decades ago, the river is ruined,
but this lone oar rowed steadily on its side
of the gunwale, bending a wake through time,
until it circled back to my hands and nudged
the boat's bow upon this far bank of memory.

To Know This Place

*Blackjack oak can withstand fire because of its thick, insulating bark and
its ability to resprout. . . . [it] is a humble, unadmired tree, but we must
also give credit to this rugged tree for living in places where few other
trees will live.*
Missouri Department of Conservation

Sawing a dead blackjack is like carving stone.
Neighbor James, an Old Woodcutter

Toss aside the tourist guide, the drug and murder novel,
and the book of nostalgic poems, then go to the blackjack
in the backyard and try to shuck its bark with those tender hands
or attempt to break a limb or twig of its sinewy self.

Study the tight-lipped lobes of its leaves and their waxed
and resistant surface and bristled tips, its half and heavily hooded acorns,
hard and bead-like, which wish to be overlooked and left to roll
into an insect hole or into a crack or crevice of drought.

Study downcast black branches hanging in tortured tangles like black-
barked lightning, and its charcoal trunk that appears to have been seared
by ancient fires, and how it doesn't deign to entertain by turning colors
or tossing in the wind, and note its refusal to be geometric

and its absolute contrast to the white clapboards, and try to plow the soil
it prefers with a shiny shoe heel—the red clay, chert, and sandstone.
If you live long enough, come view it in its death; it will be little changed,
growing only harder and harder, ever more certain of what it was.

Persimmon Tree at Leyda and Summit

I passed by several mornings
without recognizing her,
for she appears to be a cultivated
shade tree, having shaped herself
to fill a place in the lawn
and no longer hemmed in
by a grove of kinfolk who remain
back home feeding possums
and raccoons, boiling bitter jelly,
and splitting their seeds
to predict winter. But now
when meeting early mornings,
before the city people are awake
and watching, we greet
one another, discuss the weather,
study the gathering clouds,
listen for calls of a rain crow,
and avoid any mention of home.

Barn Swallows

But the quiet places . . . in this part of the country
are getting fewer and smaller.
Edsel Ford
The Ozarks Mountaineer
July 1966

The parent birds flitted
       hundreds of times
through the upper corner
       of the barn door
with mouths full
       of mud and grass
while we milked below.

Each trip seemed
       synchronized
to the blinking
       of the human eye
until the birds
       became as invisible
as the blink of an eye.

They built adobe
       nests in raftered silence,
seeking only to live
       and to raise their brood
in that high, shadowed perch.

Wild Cherry Trees

Those Old Farmers

They loomed in distant fencerows on horizons
of my childhood. The gray of many winters
seemed always to hang heavy upon them,
and their leaden silver scales of bark
found color only from the curious greens
of lichen growing there. They did not invite
children to play near them, and their limbs
were far beyond reach, and they always held
a stern, severe stillness in their branches,
withered and broken by winds of hard times.
But when brave enough to approach alone,
I sometimes sensed a sweetness concealed
under their tight and ashen exteriors
and wondered what grief made them wish
to forget this fragrant part of themselves.

Prickly Pear

It should be far southwest of these hills;
an oddity here, it must have thrown itself
flat among the rocks as glaciers retreated
to avoid being dragged away. It maintains
that instinct and presses itself to the ground
each winter and deflates and darkens
and wrinkles its pads, and, like a woodchuck,
slows its pulse and drops its body temperature
and with needled fingers clutches cast-off leaves
like an old widow clutching a faded scarf.
But in spring it rises from its leaf bed,
arching its arms, a living Stonehenge,
cupping each passing sun and pressing
that warmth into brilliant yellow blossoms,
each melting away after one day,
and then it spends the rest of summer
taking one cat-like step due south.

The Farm Youth's Companion

Death was in the cemetery of strangely named ancestors,
in old farmers with abandoned cancers on their faces,
in the family who slept through a flue fire on the first cold night of fall,
in the bloated circle of cows rounding a lightning-struck black oak,
in the ancient, shrunken great-uncle on his deathbed spitting tobacco juice
    and blood into a rusted coffee can,
in the little goats poisoned by spring grasses,
in the classmate who fell from a tractor and into his father's machine,
in the hound lost in a scent crossing a busy road,
in the remains of an old woman burning leaves alone in a long dress,
in the bullhead and bluegill minnows gulping at surface air in the last
    muddy puddle of drought,
in the blind boy who panicked while swimming and drowned his
    brother with him,
in the framed photographs of farm boys stiff in new uniforms,
in the lamb that could not nurse,
in every Sunday's soundings of vengeance and brimstone,
in young wrens and their mother swallowed into a blacksnake's darker
    night,
in the gutted deer hanging by hushed heels,
in the reclusive widow not missed for more than a month,
in the frantic, defiant cries of coyotes,
in the stillborn calf licked clean by its mother,
in prophecies of whippoorwills,
in the broken farmer hanging from a rafter.

It waited in the cottonmouth lying in the limbs over-hanging the
    swimming hole,
in the undercurrents of the flooded stream,
in the falling of a log tree,
in the rock or stob pitched by the brush hog,
in the inviting silence of the thinly frozen pond,
in the rotted floorboards of the high hay loft,
in the nest of red wasps in the corner of the machine shed,
in the spinning whispers of the power shaft,
in the science of stagnant waters,
in the screaming jealous jaws of the mother sow,
in the hunger of the wood saw,

in the cracked rung of a ladder,
in the kick of a horse or mule,
in the hay dust stored for seasons in the lung,
in the proud bull in the pasture,
in the decayed railing of the tree house,
in the depths of the hand-dug well,
in the avalanche of hay bales,
in the poisoned rust of a nail,
in the airy and comforting whirl of the mill blade.

Death was dealt to the bait in the bucket,
to the fish quivering under the blade,
to the pet steer called to slaughter by the rattle of his feed pail,
to the sack of unwanted kittens,
to an old dog led the last time to woods,
to young rabbits and mice in the freshly mown field,
to the possum in the trap,
to the water snake sunning in warm sand,
to the sinewy squirrel stripped of his skin,
to the treed raccoon,
to the frog impaled and gesticulating on the gig,
to the quail in their flush of rising,
to the chicken on the block blinking as the hatchet fell cross the sun,
to the headless, croaking chickens tossed into tall grasses to bleed and
    settle,
to the gentle, worn-out milk cow sold to market,
to the fattened hog lifting his face to the rifle, smiling.

September 15

Hershel Howerton (1935-2003)

Each year you noted summer heat would break
on or near your birthday and rains and coolness
would come. You must have noticed this when
a boy on the farm, and such awareness bred
other awareness until you could read any turn
of wind, translate notes of crickets and rain crows
and tree frogs, and foresee weather building
beyond the horizons. You have been gone
sixteen years, a parting we did not see coming,
and each day and night the wind and skies
remind me of you and remind me
that each day, regardless of the weather,
will bring joys you did not bother to predict
because you knew they would be there.

Farm Journal: Haiku Sequence

out of the city,   surprised by the sound   of my footsteps

barn door—   opening and closing   for the wind

old pony—   breath frozen white   in whiskers

walking back,   my old snowprints   belong to a stranger

falling through   the barn roof,   stars and moon

shifting fog,   a crow fades   his call remains

heron and I   standing   still

new moon,   fish share their pond   with every star

wild ivy,   after cutting it for years   she lets it grow

snake in the shed,   her garden tools lie   in the rain

bullfrog,   with each breath   summer deepens

heat wave—   her concrete chickens   stand in the shade

setting early   in the cracked window   late summer sun

in my mailbox   again today   only that same brown leaf

i turn out my lamp   the moon jumps   through my window

The Fencerow

The history of his farm
is chronicled in this fencerow
where remnants of ancient white oak
posts—posts he split when he
was young and too poor
to afford any other—
hang gray and shrunken
held by rusted steeples
to brittle two-barbed wire.
Others, added a decade later
and split by a young neighbor
who had a family and needed work,
have also rotted from the ground.
Steel posts mark his mid-life,
when he could afford them
and was thinking ahead to the day
he could no longer walk the line
and drive posts. Five strands
of heavy gauge barbed wire
were also stretched then,
and even now they have the polish
of galvanization upon them;
then came death along the fencerow,
and the sumac returned,
and multi-flora rose, and the cedars,
some of which are now thicker
than his arms when he died.

Turkey Buzzards

Throughout summer they roosted
in a dead oak on my neighbor's
back acreage, and now in November
their relations flock in, congregating,
contemplating a move farther south.
Their sleeping quarters and coasting
circles grow crowded, yet they hesitate
to leave town—perhaps the rent
is paid up to the end of the month,
or they are waiting for Uncle Baldy's
brood to glide in. Most likely,
this lingering warm weather
and their rare avian sense of smell
has convinced them that the season
of death has not ended, and I
see them each morning perched
on bare limbs, their dreaded red
and raw faces facing first rays,
and, since granted no voice to sing,
they hold wings half raised, accepting
with silent grace the grace given.

Gerry Sloan

Sassafras
Sassafras albidum

Photo by Chris Moore

Gerry Sloan

I was born in Oklahoma City in 1947 and moved to rural Leflore County shortly thereafter, ranging freely between the houses of grandparents in Howe and Heavener until my father bought a house on the G. I. Bill. I attended elementary school in Heavener through sixth grade. The Heavener Runestone made a permanent impression, as if you could inscribe characters in a wilderness where people might later puzzle over their meaning. Maybe that was my first poetic inspiration. My Sunday school teacher, Gloria Farley, wrote the definitive book on the Heavener Runestone. My paternal grandfather taught me to fish at age four, because I was the only grandchild who could sit still. I feel fishing and verse have much in common, including observation, patience, and perseverance.

My family border-hopped for four generations between Oklahoma and Arkansas, many of them buried in rural Crawford County, Arkansas, including my 2G grandfather who was "killed by the bushwhackers." My father was hired by the Shipley Baking Company, and we moved to Fort Smith in 1958. That same year I attended Scout camp on the Buffalo River and was "hooked," you might say, on the Ozarks. I was fortunate in having an English teacher named John Taylor in high school, who turned me on to literature and introduced me to the work of Vance Randolph. My poetry was first published in *The Litsmith*, the high school literary magazine, and the *Southwest Times Record*. I would often spend my lunch money at Vivian's Bookshop. Those books still collect dust in my study: *Words for the Wind* by

Theodore Roethke, *The Collected Poems of Stephen Crane*, and a collection of haiku published in Tokyo.

At Arkansas Tech I pursued a BA degree, majoring in music with an English minor. I discovered facsimile editions of William Blake's prophetic books in the school library. B. C. Hall taught some writing courses and helped me with my poetry. James Whitehead offered me an assistantship at the U of A that proved to be Frost's "road not taken." I chose instead to attend Northwestern University in Chicago for a master's degree in music.

Recently retired from teaching music for 43 years at the University of Arkansas, I sit on my hill in Fayetteville observing the profound changes happening (some too quickly) to our region as well as globally. Many of my poems are meditations on these changes. I have published five chapbooks and two collections: *Paper Lanterns* (2011) and *Crossings: A Memoir in Verse* (2017). Some of my first literary inspirations were the New England Transcendentalists, especially Emerson and Thoreau. So, if I had to label myself, I would choose to be remembered as an "Ozarks Transcendentalist."

Most of my poems are self-explanatory, but a few glosses may be in order. The faux epigraph for "Grandmother Gourd" was cobbled from a much longer scientific report. The T. S. Eliot epigraph for "Layers" is from the sequence entitled "East Coker" in *Four Quartets*. It is one of my many non-sonnets, which allude to that tradition while ignoring most of the rules.

Danzón is a Cuban social dance from the early 20th century, and my "Danzón" is probably a gesture to commemorate my five years in a salsa band. "Ode Ending with a Line by Roethke" is another of my so-called *décimas*, 10-line poems which have little resemblance to their Spanish forebear, a competitive improvised form that strictly rhymes. "Danzón" adheres to a rhyme scheme; otherwise, my use of rhyme is more often spontaneous, though I have to beware of my tendency to end with a rhymed couplet (probably residue from the Shakespearean sonnet).

The minimalist "Ode" below is with tongue in cheek, since Keats's odes were sometimes ten pages or longer. The allusion to "Nanook hooking a walrus" is from Flaherty's early documentary, *Nanook of the North* (1922), the Hemingway reference is to his novella *The Old Man and the Sea*. The last line is from "The Waking," a villanelle by Theodore Roethke, another early influence, though I switch pronouns in the quote ("we" instead of "I").

The line in "Swallows" alludes to a book title (*The Amazing Zhang Women*) at the Nelson-Atkins Museum, where I took my Chinese daughter when she was still in high school. Her family name is Zhang, so I referred to her thereafter as "my amazing Zhang woman." "Howl for Susan Powell" is for a poet friend who was invited to be guest of honor when Yellowstone reintroduced wolves in the 1990s. Another non-sonnet, it gently pokes fun at Ginsberg's epic from the 1950s (initially called "Howl for Carl Solomon") by referencing an actual "howl" from Susan's pet wolf, Kegan. I was reassured it was a gesture of rare distinction.

"Why France Sold Us Louisiana" is largely history as slapstick, based on the catalog of horrors from chapter two ("La Salle's Luck") of Bob Lancaster's *The Jungles of Arkansas* (University of Arkansas Press, 1989). "Rock-Skipping on the West Fork" is possibly my response to a Miller Williams poem I admire, his "Poem for Emily" which appeared in *Poetry Magazine* shortly after the birth of his granddaughter. Unfortunately, Miller passed away a few years before the age forecast in the poem. So when I turned 67, I summoned my son back from Minnesota and hurried to skip stones on the White River. After all these years, he still kicked my butt. Like Miller's poem, mine also scans and rhymes. Though rhyming is now out of fashion (except in hiphop), it's one of my few poems I can recite from memory. It also echoes my lifelong admiration for Emily Dickinson.

In closing, it makes me happy that more than half these poems lack a first-person pronoun. I enjoy escaping my ego and slipping into nature, placing our human foibles in a larger frame, beyond calendar time and into geological time ("Grandmother Gourd," "Layers," and "Double Exposure"), not just hoping for transcendence but for a kind of redemption as well.

Thaw

After intense extended cold, wildlife
begins to re-emerge, hesitantly
at first, then more boldly
reclaiming their turf.

Then a whitetail deer appears,
alertly reconnoitering the hill,
tweaking an ear at the sound
of two gray squirrels playing
chase at the base of an oak.

A bevy of birds takes turns
at the neighbors' feeder, still
chastened by recent weather,
their ongoing territorial dispute
for the moment seemingly moot,
sensing a welcome return to order
here on necessity's fragile border.

Grandmother Gourd
(for Soraya and Luciya)

Curcubita pepo ozarkana, the Ozark wild gourd (aka Johnny gourd)
was probably cultivated by First Nations people some 3000 years
ago, to produce the variety of squash and gourds we know today.
                    Smithsonian News Service, November, 1992

Climbing the limestone bluffs
overlooking Beaver Lake,
my teenage granddaughters and I
discover a patch of wild gourds

near the end of their growing season,
some already yellowing for seed.
They must have fed the people who
quarried these ancient chert nodules

for stone tools, like the scrapers we find
along the lake margin, now revealed
by the late December sun
amidst dry leaves and driftwood.

It's almost as if our predecessors
still communicate non-verbally,
their messages spread botanically
before us on bluffs and fence-rows,

a cuneiform of tenacious vines
that struggle to survive us,
if only we have eyes to see,
if we only take time to notice.

Layers

"The houses are all gone under the sea.
The dancers are all gone under the hill."
                                    T. S. Eliot

Before, this suburban subdivision
was a strawberry patch (I remember
it well), and before that was a woodland
meadow (before my time), and before that
was a small forest cleared by weary settlers
marking their trek through the wilderness.
And judging from the fossils in protruding
limestone knees, it was once a shallow sea
where mud-sharks ruled the food chain.
                              And before
that was something molten, without form,
inconceivable to those who scribble
sonnets without rhyme, those who slam
their doors and then depart for work in cars,
peeling back the layers and layers of darkness.

Greenhouse Addendum

Leafbuds on the mulberry tree
are confused by the April snow,
not knowing whether to
come out and freeze, or hold back
a few more days. Fingertips bursting
with chlorophyll, they reach out to read
the wind's icy braille
and the intent of a sky
whose mood has grown glacial.
Air currents once predictable
roam the globe like riderless
horses. The car keys
jingle in my pocket
like coffin nails.

The Star That Got Its Wish

The season's first wet snow produces
snowmen by the hundreds, whole
families in many yards,
going about their business
with carrot noses, pebble
eyes, mimicking us
passers-by
with token caps
and scarves. It's hard to tell
if they are waving hello
or goodbye. Tonight
the clouds will
disappear. The crescent moon and Pleiades
will glisten their approval, knowing
tomorrow a brighter star
must pass by here,
calling its crystalline
children home.

Danzón

Dry leaves dancing down the street
lack the necessary feet
to race this far ahead of me,
trusting the wind's choreography
to send them where they need to be.

Only we humans second-guess
our choices, then curse or bless
the outcome, the outside chance
that maybe time and circumstance
will teach our clumsy feet to dance.

Ode Ending with a Line by Roethke

A small red spider has captured a fly
three times its size, swings in the wind
on a single sparkling strand of gossamer,
enough food to last its brood for a week.
This could be Nanook hooking a walrus,

or Hemingway's lone fisherman
unable to land his trophy catch.
But here the wind is unrelenting,
tossing them willy-nilly to-and-fro.
We learn by going where we have to go.

Osage Orange
(for Rick Squires)

Does the spider know its gossamer web
mimics the whorled rings of your wood,
the former evanescent as air, the latter
so hard that pioneers used you
for making fence-posts? Is anyone aware

that your apparent disproportion
reflects The Golden Mean, observed once
by the ancients, the laws of symmetry
highly overrated? Can anybody guess
the secrets etched into your grain?

Double Exposure

Fossil starfish in Ozark caves
once drifted beneath
an inland sea,
its beachcombers now
a band of stumbling spelunkers

who glimpse the familiar pentagram,
evoking as it does the head
and four limbs of man,
or the five-alarm Fire Pink
flaming soundlessly aboveground.

Centipede

We could not have been more astonished
if Dad's uncle had arrived with a caged
tiger instead of the eight-inch centipede
in a quart fruit jar, threatening with its alien
black body and Halloween-orange legs

that doubled as stingers. It's fate I can't recall—
science-fair project or death in a dumpster—
though now it must suffer the fate of all
the Big Fish stories and Big Snake stories
that vanish on the tongues of the tellers.

Windows

Reflective surfaces can be deadly. / The migratory bird whose ancient password / is denied by tempered glass. / The mayfly whose concentric ripples / on the fractured mirror of a pond

are written invitations to hungry carp. / Or this poem, which may not reflect thinking / so much as it creates a space for thought, / just one of a million windows / on our flightpath.

Poem at the Solstice

Yesterday a pair of bald eagles
soared over the Arkansas River,
an unprecedented sight during all
the years I've been crossing there.
Today a sundog in the western sky
revealed not the usual auspicious arc
but a smaller swatch of the color-wheel
we once learned in elementary school.
In a few hours the full moon will clear
the horizon like a sterling-silver platter
serving a meal of invisible filaments
in spite of the unpredictable weather.
Were we not too distracted to notice,
earthly beauty would be hard to bear.

Swallows
(for Wanna)

Villagers in southern China
leave a window open
throughout the year
if swallows build their nests
high in the rafters,
considering it an omen
of great good fortune.

But here in Arkansas
we're more likely to call
the exterminator, ignorant
of signifiers, clueless how
in the house you own
in a faceless subdivision,
swallows have singled you

out for recognition, another
"amazing Zhang woman,"
built their nest directly
above your front door,
until their fledglings
exit and leave their
adobe imprimatur.

Shadows of Mount Sequoyah

Dana Tiger taught me how to say
the word "cedar" in Cherokee. It
tangled my Aryan tongue at first,
so I practiced until it felt natural.

Passing my arboreal elder tonight,
I say "a-tsi-na" aloud then repeat,
certain it hears and can understand
the sound we humans once assigned

to an aging sentinel guarding our hill.
I'm sure it will be here after I'm gone,
still anchoring its thin layer of topsoil,
still bending its gnarly arms in the wind.

Though I have the gift of mobility,
I probably wouldn't notice if you
cut me off at the knees, my roots
left behind years ago in Oklahoma.

Grandad would sit in the summer shade
carving talismans out of red cedar,
leaving them scattered about the yard
to be deciphered a lifetime later.

Howl for Susan Powell
(with a big shoutout to Kegan)

The she-wolf in your dooryard
howls twice through the fence
as if in tentative acceptance
if not forgiveness for crimes
against her kind committed
by mine, those vagrant forebears
who crossed the Atlantic and finally
blundered into the Ozarks where we
offered steep bounties on wolf "scalps"
for nearly two centuries. Therefore she
lifts her snout to the sky and delivers
a shout so primal it defies description,
warns and welcomes simultaneously,
testing whether I be friend or enemy.

Why France Sold Us Louisiana

La Salle led some wannabe colonists
through the region we know as Texas,
most of their time spent hungry or lost.
They "lived on mud turtles and the occasional
buffalo while feeding rattlesnakes to their hogs"*

and broke ground with rudimentary plows,
hoping to grow something edible. Meanwhile
some died of venereal disease, picked up
in Hispaniola. And one man died
from eating a prickly pear. The priest

was gored by an irate buffalo. One
poor soul was eaten by an alligator.
Their leader veered between lucidity
and psychotic episodes. His nephew
and several others were eventually

axe-murdered in their sleep
by a disgruntled faction, La Salle himself
ambushed after finding their bodies,
the survivors escaping to either be
enslaved or killed by the Indians.

*Bob Lancaster

The Fox

He crosses the road with his tail
straight out, moving purposefully.
Our headlights reveal a ghostly
beard—a baby hare or a quail—

suspended from the set chin.
It's hard to see why he disturbs
our sleep within the suburbs,
or know how he'll survive when

the last pasture is paved over
with parking lots and manicured
green lawns, the distinction blurred
between who's prey and predator.

All the wiles of Kingdom Come
will not preserve you, Brother Fox,
from that rude pestilence which knocks
at both our doorways, waiting, dumb.

Nature Channel

You hesitate above the cluttered TV tray.
The coyotes have come once more for the baby elk.

The mother stands her ground for as long as possible,
pausing between rounds to lick the baby's face.

She knows, deep down, this signifies goodbye.
There are five of them and only one of her.

Patiently they circle the doomed pair
in this ancient game whose rules are foreknown.

And time, like some wind-up automaton, some
merciless predictable rerun, seems always on their side.

Rock-Skipping on the West Fork
(for Brady)

Semis grind to make the grade
    behind us on the hill;
otherwise the summer stream
    is somnolent and still.

Already, son, your arm is strong,
    your aim as straight as mine,
even though I'm thirty-eight
    and you are only nine.

Someday, when you're thirty-eight
    and I am sixty-seven,
I hope that we can come back here
    like truants under heaven

to skip the stones that weighed us down
    in years less kind than these,
and watch them clear the opposite shore
    and vanish into the trees.

Assisi Is Everywhere

The wren comes near then surprises me by hopping on my bare feet,
seated here on the lower deck in my easy chair—an unprecedented
gesture to be sure. A "visitation" my daughter calls it.

Maybe this is how Saint Francis felt before becoming a lawn ornament,
to be thus affirmed with unblinking trust. To be so singled out.

But as I watch the wren splash in the birdbath with such unabashed
pleasure, I wonder if he is my teacher, sent here for life instruction
tuition-free, the same way I descend from my flimsy limb for this
cleansing baptism—this poetry.

Mark Spitzer

Sweetgum
Liquidambar styraciflua

Mark Spitzer

Mark Spitzer is the author of thirty-plus books, including *GLURK! A Hellbender Odyssey* (Anaphora Literary Press), *Crypto-Arkansas* (Spuyten Duyvil), and several environmental fish books published by the university presses of Nebraska, Arkansas, and North Texas. He is the editor in chief of the avant-garde poetry series Toad Suck Éditions and has been a professor of creative writing at Truman State University and the University of Central Arkansas with a specialization in poetry and creative nonfiction. Spitzer was last seen hiking in the Missouri Ozarks in search of the Nixa Hellhound. For more information, visit sptzr.net.

Numerous legendary cryptozoological creatures have found fertile ground to evolve in the Ozarks, and Mark Spitzer has made it his mission to explore and research such phenomena. He looks for the stories behind the stories, then reports his findings via the Postmodern technique of investigative poetics, an American literary tradition which finds its roots in the work of Ezra Pound, Charles Olson, William Carlos Williams, and Ed Sanders. Through a scholarly and not unbiased collaging of history, folklore, biology, journalism, politics, imagery, and literary truncations from myriad texts, Spitzer's exposés on hoop snakes, wampus cats, the Ozark Howler, the enigmatic blue humans of Blowing Cave, the mythological Blue Man of Spring Creek, and Oklahoma Octopi are documented in free verse with direct citations and commentary gained from first-person fieldwork. These studies and others will soon be available in his forthcoming collection of monster-themed mysteries entitled *Cryptozarkia.*

Spitzer's contributions to this anthology include an overview of the horrible Green Gowrow, a primitive cave-dwelling reptile which allegedly threatened nineteenth-century pioneer culture in Arkansas; a breakdown of how the spirit of a missing professor from Kansas injected itself into a specific genus of rock bass; a primer on an infamous, mutant alligator gar that marauded and menaced its way into a communal consciousness; a summarization of how man-eating catfish narratives from ye olde Europe found a new form in the mountains of Missouri; and excerpts from his epic poem *GLURK!*, which studies in depth the tragic demise of and recovery efforts for North America's largest, fugliest salamander.

As for thoughts about writing, Spitzer advises getting off one's butt and getting out there, getting lost, getting in trouble, losing one's cellphone in the woods, and hunting down those in the know for further perspectives that illuminate lost gems. He advises using the tools of trial and error, self-denigration, screwing up, and banging one's head against one's desk to muck one's way out of a morass and unto higher ground.

Mythology of the Terrible Green Gowrow

Throughout the Ozarks
   there are tales of cavern-dwelling lizards
     reaching lengths of twenty feet
       carrying their young marsupially
        and laying eggs
          the size of kegs
            while terrorizing communities

       back in 1897
         Little Rock businessman Bill Miller
           formed a posse in Searcy County
             to catch a pesky reptile
               responsible for slaughtering hogs
                                    dogs
                                    cats
                                  and cattle

on the outskirts of Blanco near Calf Creek Township
   following tracks with Winchesters
     they discovered a cave
       filled with grinning skulls
       and then it erupted
       from the river:

     "a huge body of a sickly green hue"
       with "two enormous tusks"
         webbed feet complete with claws
        "enormous scales"
          spined stegasaurously
         and "a sharp bone"
         sickling forth
          from its tail

"GOWROW! GOWROW!"
　　roared the horrible
　　　green gowrow
　　　　of the goofus family
　　　　　as it stomp-waddled toward the men
　　　　　　shaking the terrain
　　　　　　　like a stern-wheeled steamer
　　　　　　　　or in other accounts
　　　　　　　　　"the San Francisco earthquake"

Miller took a photograph
　　which was published as an illustration
　　　by Elmer Burrus
　　　　and written up by Elbert Smithee
　　　　　in the *Arkansas Gazette*
　　　　　　recalling how the farmers
　　　　　　　fired on its "ponderous"
　　　　　　　　man-shaped head

　　& how it lashed its dragon tail
　　　slicing down trees
　　　　plus the leg right off
　　　　　"a poor fellow named Tom Brennan"　　　(January 31, 1897)

　　　　　then hitting the monster
　　　　　　with another volley
　　　　　　　they sprang upon the beast
　　　　　　　　and chopped it into chunks

Miller proclaimed it a pachyderm hybrid
     fused from a *hyaenida* and *rhinnocerotidae*
          dating back to the Miocene
               so sent its skin and skeleton
                    on to the Smithsonian

                              —but guess what?
                                   it never arrived

          shades of Vance Randolph's
               folklore of the Missourian
                    who captured a gowrow by enticing it
                         to eat a wagonload of dried apples
                              which caused it to swell up
                                   in its burrow

               the Missourian pitched a tent over it
                    and charged 25 cents admission
                         but before the paid-up patrons could enter
                         a shredded showman staggered out
                              bleeding and screaming
                                   "THE GOWROW BROKE OUT!
                                   RUN FOR YOUR LIVES!"

                    then rattle of chains and banging pans
                         women screaming, tent collapsing
                              and the crowd took off
                                   and nobody got
                                        their money back
                                        (*We Always Lie to Strangers*, 1951)

shades also of the Devil's Hole
     near the village of Self in Boone County
          where landowner E. J. Rhodes (no date known)
               lowered himself into a fissure
                    dropped 200 feet
                         toward a commotion
                              but refused to spelunk
                                   any further

Clio Harper and co.
   of Little Rock, though
      picked up where Rhodes left off
      circa 1924

         lowering a flat iron
            into the hissing hole
               something happened at 200 feet
               they pulled up the rope
               the handle was bent

            so they lowered a stone
               and something snapped
               severing the line

               they tried it again
               same thing
                  bite marks
                  "discernable"
                                    (*Rayburn's Ozark Guide,*
                                       Summer 1949)

so I went to the storied Devil's Hole
   clearly marked on Google Earth
      got onto the farmer's land
         and found a sinkhole
            stuffed with the stuff of dumps:

            bald tires, window screens
               exercise bikes, washing machines
               kitchen sinks, brush cuttings
               and a bright pink bowling ball

            in other words:
               a giant pile of
                  irrefutable
                     but colorful
                        Arkansas
                        garbage.

Goggle-Eye Gobbledygook

According to *Rayburn's Ozark Guide*
a publication that used to print
"tall tales or other bits of lore"   (Spring 1951)
there was this professor from Kansas
who went fishing on the Buffalo River
around 1917

now this old boy
had mongo "shell rim spectacles"
and he hooked himself "a fish so large
that he could not land it"
so he hung on and it
pulled him in

Yep   even to this day
folks have seen the professor
being dragged up and down the river
still clinging to
his fishing pole

but wait   there's more
because suddenly there was
a new fish in town:

    Ambloplites rupestris
a non-native member of
      the sunfish family
built like a cross between
a bream and a bass
with one distinguishing
notable feature:

    big ol' bubble eyes
just like that missing professor
with his thicker than baloney
        bifocals
        and refusal to let go

so now his haint inhabits the streams
of northeast Arkansas
where an introduced species
commonly known as "goggle-eye"
                and/or "red eye"
is believed to exist because
                        "all such fish
                        had seen the professor"   (Spring 1947)

in an area   by the way
that just happened to be stocked
with this specific
northern rock bass
        (which differs from the Ozark
        and shadow bass)

spawned in a hatchery
        "established in Neosho, Missouri"   (Cashner and Suttkus, 1978)
        à la 1888

So is it a coincidence
that most federal stocking activities
take decades for breeding
populations to take

or is it a fact that
    "great numbers of fish
        soon appeared in the river. . .
        with protruding eyes,
        resembling . . . the Kansas professor"?   (*Ozark Guide*, Spring 1947)

Well   Will Rice of St. Joe would know
because he's the reporter
who recorded the legend of this fish
            among other
            questionable
            contentions

ie
"a turtle killed in the Buffalo River . . .
which 'made a meal for forty families,
with two barrels of soup left over'"   (*We Always Lie to Strangers*, 69)

or
the killer turnips that erupted from a shed
murdering a herd of cows . . .   (*Ibid.*, 90)

or get this
"a man on [the] Buffalo River
who 'grabbed a big frog by the leg.
[which] jumped clear across the river
with him hanging on'"   (*Ibid.*, 71)

Let it be known   however
that Will Rice "was best known . . . for his sly humor.
                He didn't think of his yarns as tall tales,
                but liked to consider them
                'things that are always possible—
                but not always very probable'"
                                (*Arkansas Gazette*, April 6, 1953)
in his own words
Will Rice of St. Joe wrote
        "I always enjoyed seeing the town's name . . .
        so I began sending items from here
        just to see 'St. Joe' in print"

    adding
        "Sometimes, perhaps,
        I would help the item out . . .
        to make it more entertaining
        and to insure a wider circulation"
                                (*Arkansas Democrat Sunday
                                Magazine*, July 18, 1948)
So no wonder a year
after documenting this rise
            in goggle-eyes
Rice recycled his own
fishy fish story

"about the phantom fisherman . . .
    a determined looking professor from Kansas
    with . . . horn-rimmed glasses"
            who hooked a catfish in Arkansas
            weighing 400 pounds
            et cetera

        so now his ghost sits fishing there
and they say that during electrical storms
            "the haunted fisherman throws
            fish over his shoulder
            and the person who happens to be there
            can fill a basket"   (*Arkansas Democrat Sunday Magazine,*
                                                        April 11, 1948)

Anyway
that's the news from St. Joe
where the apparitions of imaginations
            still hold to claims made
by dubious Ozark storytellers

like those who spin yarns
of goggle-eyed perch
infused with the spirit
of a stubborn professor
            still being towed
            up and down the Buffalo River

an unlikely story
that keeps getting told

        one way
or another.

Big Al: The Name Remains

As Ernest Dewcy wrote
in an article entitled
      "A Lot of Strange Creatures
        Are Lying About the Ozarks Area":

      "It has been noted that
      sterility of the soil
      has a strong tendency
      to increase fertility
        of the imagination"   *(The Hutchinson News-Herald*
               May 13, 1951)

which accounts for legends like Big Al
a monstrous alligator gar
native to the White River
and allegedly not
      a "'natural' gar at all,
      but some kind of a demon
      in disguise"   *(We Always Lie to Strangers*, 207)

but the thing is
rumors of this "immortal . . .
         supernatural"   *(Ibid.* 206)
           thirty foot
           gargantugar

originated in the fields fringing
the Arkansas and Mississippi river valleys
from Natchez to Little Rock
following Reconstruction

still
not much is known
about this crypto boogey creature
other than it's been reported
      "to have killed many swimmers"
and was especially fond
      "of Negro children"

as Vance Randolph notes
        "when a young woman mysteriously disappeared
        the neighbors used to say
        'Big Al must have got her,'
        meaning that she had run off
        with a stranger."   (*Ibid.*, 207)

about the only other literal mention
                        of this mystery fish
is in a Baptist college honors thesis
that studied folk narratives
as constructs of communities

its author Sharon Hibbard states:
        "The folktale arises from a need
        experienced at a certain stage of development
        in human society.
        It is the circumstances
        which generate a folktale,
        which form its conception
        its shape,
        and its narrative style;
        as long as these circumstances prevail,
        the folktale will endure"   ("Folklore: A Study and
                                        Tales from the Ozarks," 1975)
But the story of Big Al
did not endure
        it fizzled away
        with nary a trace

though one thing remained
a name whose legacy can be found
        in American mobsters
Big Al Bruno and Big Al Capone

and numerous athletes and musicians
not to mention professional wrestlers
        comedians and
race car drivers

there's also Big Al
the fossilized Allosaurus
Big Al the mascot
for Alabama's Crimson Tide
and Big Al's strip club
the first topless bar
in the USA

and let's not forget
Big Gay Al from *South Park*
Big Al as code for Alzheimer's
and a renowned
           thousand pound
                  Big Al
                    igator in Texas

but there are also plenty massive fish
with this lasting moniker
like the loveable lunker in Andrew Clements's
bestselling children's book
Big Al   (Simon & Schuster, 1997)

plus a famous "neurotic" triggerfish
at Boston's New England Aquarium
who made national news
when it outgrew
its tank   (proquest-om.ucark.idm.oclc.org/central/docview/
                   2688122662F03F7427D054668PQ/)

then there's the iconic champion bass
worth fifteen thousand cash
at the annual Forrest Wood Cup
Fishing Contest in Hot Springs
who "has only been caught once
        in 2017"   (*Arkansas Democrat-Gazette*
                         August 5, 2018)

So what do all these larger than life
mystical and mythical
Big Als have in common
other than the adjectives
just listed?

Answer:
as Higgins wrote
folk tales arise
from societal needs

like the need to create
        scapegoats
        saviors
         magical muses

whatever we need
that's bigger than us
stronger than us

and powerful enough
        to bullshit all
the bullshit away.

Old Blue Possibilities

As *Time Magazine* reported in the thirties
the "Biggest catfish in the world is Old Blue
    who inhabits the Missouri River
    and is so big he once got stuck
    trying to go through a canal lock"   (August 17, 1931)

hence a plethora of narratives
of divers delving under dams
encountering mega
mutant cats

primarily
Old Blue who
Vance Randolph contends
lived in the Osage River
"for at least fifty years"   (*We Always Lie to Strangers*, 216)

such that
even after that system was dammed
the stories continued

particularly those
of a "well-known Osage River boatman"
named Jerry English
who made it his mission
to catch the lauded lunkercat that

according to Skunk Hide Turner
and M. N. White of Warsaw M.O.
once jumped "the Bagnell Dam
    and traveled all the way to Louisville"   (*Ibid.*, 217)

Robert Gilmore on the other hand
refers to Old Blue's removal
from Lake of the Ozarks
which caused the water level to drop
    "18 feet,
      leaving docks, marinas
      and boats stranded"   (*OzarksWatch*, vol. IV, no. 3, 1991)

such cock and bull   of course
has roots in journalism
dating back to the journals of
Lewis and Clark

who recorded a "large 'white' catfish,
                    undoubtedly [a] blue . . .
                    reaching 1.5 m in length"
                                        (American Fisheries Society Symposium
                                                        proceedings, 1999)
a solid possibility given
that sixty years later
a "blue channel cat" was documented
    "just below Portland, Missouri"
    weighing "315 lb"   (Heckmann, 1950)

mucho reports of unlikely blues
then followed from St. Joe
where the skeleton of
a cat named Turntable Jack
was found on a sandbar in 1899
measuring "14 feet from head to tail"

to the lower Osage where
        "several old rivermen . . . estimated its weight
        in the neighborhood of 500 pounds"   (*Missouri Conservationist,*
                                                        June 1947)
to Little Rock
        (a cat so huge that it contained
        a "200-pound catfish, three fat hogs,
        a yoke of oxen and
        an acre of burnt woods")   (*We Always Lie to Strangers,* 214)

a tradition which continued
into the twenty first century
when Kato "Mudcat" Mudger
supposedly captured
a "736-pound . . . Mekong giant catfish"
in the Mississippi River

but the photo of this fish
containing "a size 37 boot"
is clearly a flathead
whose eyes would be smaller
if this wasn't a blatant act
of sloppy Photoshoppery

(RiverBender.com)

(note how shadows don't match
directions of light on man and fish)

But what if we didn't have
all these plausibilities
for Old Blue and
his behemoth brethren?

And who would we be
if we didn't continue
ye old Euro tradition
of embellishing jumbo
man-eating catfish?

Well   if you ask me
we wouldn't be we
we would be
unwe

        which ain't a possibility
so why even consider
adjusting our nature
when Nature basically
made us this way?

Just like Old Blue
                who
according to the Kansas City *Star*
has been known to stick
                "his head out of the water"
                and wink
                "his left eye"   (January 8, 1941)

thereby leaving
the question to consider:
                at who
                and why?

Excerpts from "*GLURK!*" from *GLURK! A Hellbender Odyssey*

VII. 2014 Ozark Hellbender Fest
Pocahontas, AR

we camped in the old settlement park
then drove into town
saw the famous asteroid
and made our way
to the square

the first place we stopped
was a run-down junk shop
that used to be the local brothel
they had plow parts, jars of jam
and an antique cathode ray machine

but they also had one remaining
"SAVE THE HELLBENDER" t-shirt
made in Spain
which I bought

Armadillo Jeff was pumped to run
the annual Hellbender 5K
but there was no registration tent

also
the hellbender lecture had been canceled
because of the recent F4
that wiped out the Game & Fish Commish
down in Central Arkansas

and there was no Hellbender Auction this year
and there was no Hellbender Boogie Dice Biker Run
but across from the old courthouse
there was a dumpy lumpy
sculpture of one

so we saw the quilts
we bypassed the clogs
and went to the Randolph County
Historical Museum

to see the jumbo gator gar
it was seven feet long w/ yellowed fins
from being displayed for sixty years

which made this trip
almost worth it.

LXVII

The US Fish & Wildlife boat
finally bags a robust male
which they can tell
from its rosy vent
so the boats converge
for "processing"

Jeronimo works it
free of its swaddlings
brings forth a wavy mass
of black & brown calico
a living, squiggling
lasagna-lizard
screaming from a wide
        red
         Kermit mouth
    gleaming a line
     of thin little teeth

also noticeable
are tiny pink toes
gripping and flailing

like a baby
a human baby
which Capt. K
for some reason
            dubs
"Sparky."

LXVIII

the Game and Fish
PIT tag scanner
is out of whack
but Captain K figures
Sparky's a "recap"

"Looks like he's been snipped before"
            he tells the crew
pointing to some spots on Sparky's swinging
oar of a tail
which he tries to use
to leverage himself
from Jeronimo's Latex grip

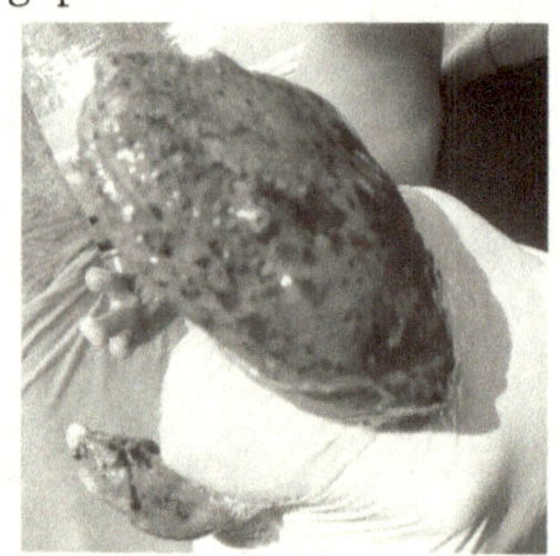

Sparky's then placed
into a Tupperware
where looking down
at gossamer streamers
ghosting white phlegm
I ask if this is the slime
that gets released
when a salamander thinks
it's a goner

a gluiness I've felt before
with mud puppies
 excreting secretions
 when pierced for bait

"Yep," Captain K says, "that's the stuff
it's a really sticky substance"

"Is it really toxic?
          I ask
Capt. K laughs
and goes into a story
about some guy who couldn't be outdone
so when he heard some dude
was dared to taste some hellbender slime
he went and licked a full-grown adult
from slimy head
to slimy tail

"Then spent the next hour
spitting in the river
and washing his mouth"
          Captain K tells us

needless to say
none of us feel the burning urge
to pass Sparky around
and take a hit.

Agnes Vojta

Bur Oak
Quercus macrocarpa

Photo by Thomas Vojta

Agnes Vojta

I grew up in East Germany. My childhood dreams were to be either a writer or an opera singer, but I ended up becoming a physicist. The Berlin Wall fell when I was in college, and that opened the world. I lived a few years in California, Oregon, and England, and then my family moved to Rolla, Missouri, where I teach physics at Missouri University of Science and Technology. Immediately after we arrived here, we bought a couple of hiking guidebooks and began exploring the Ozarks. After emigrating to the U. S., I struggled with the loss of my home culture and was unable to write for a long time. It took over ten years until I was finally able to resume writing poetry, now in English. Exploring the Ozarks, becoming familiar with a new landscape, and finally being able to write about it, helped me feel at home.

I love sharing poetry and songs at readings and performances. My first collection *Porous Land* was published in 2019, *The Eden of Perhaps* followed in 2020, and *A Coracle for Dreams* was released in the spring of 2022, all by Spartan Press. My poems have appeared in a variety of magazines, and you can find selections on my website, agnesvojta.com. My collaborative project with the painter Greg Edmondson, titled *Dark Matter,* was on exhibit at the Smalter Gallery in Kansas City in the spring of 2022.

Writing is my way of dealing with the impermanence of being. With my poems, I try to capture images and sensations that are fleeting. I want to preserve them in words, to revisit and share. Poetry helps me orient myself in the world. Writing also means to bear witness, to create community by finding words for shared human experience.

I write a lot about nature. Nature often gives me the metaphor that expresses what I cannot otherwise put into words, teaches me lessons that extend into other areas of life, and mirrors my interior landscape. I need to be in the wilderness for my physical and mental health. Even in times of greatest stress, one day of the weekend is sacred, and I spend it in the woods or on the river. Spending time in nature is a spiritual practice for me, my way of meditating. On an easy trail or river, you can let the thoughts wander and percolate; difficult terrain requires intense concentration that forces you to be completely in the moment in a way few other experiences do. Getting away from the chatter of civilization and connecting with nature grounds me and puts everything into perspective. The wilderness speaks a deep truth that surpasses what we try to grasp intellectually, and when I can hear those voices, I feel balanced, connected, and at peace. Being a poet has affected the way I see; I find myself observing more closely and being more attentive.

Witch Hazel

I have not written
in a long time,
there's too much to say,
and I do not know
where to begin.

Let me just tell you
what I did today.
I fed the cat, sat
with my coffee cup,
watched the sun rise.

I went to the woods.
It was cold. I found
frost flowers at noon
under the deep blue
Ozark winter sky.

I walked by the creek
to the old mill, little
more than a shack.
The water rushed
down red rhyolite rocks,

and the witch hazel
have started to bloom.
They smell so lovely.
I hope they are blooming
where you are, too.

Celebrating the Thaw

Pale pink, the moon
sinks toward the horizon.
Mists are rising.
Fields dream of spring.

In shallow pools,
the peepers shrill the air.
Steps crunch the grass.
The frogs fall silent—all

but one: defiant, he keeps singing
a series of melodious notes,
audacious soloist who won't contain
his joie de vivre.

Burning Brush

The embers still
dream beneath ash.

A breeze tickles
small flames awake—

they flicker
like laughter.

Status Report

I walked along my creek
which is a term of endearment—
one doesn't own a creek any more
than one owns the clouds—

stood on a limestone slab
and watched the ripples on the water,
the reflection of leafless trees,
the darting minnows.

I moved an earthworm
from the path onto the grass.
The robins were eating red berries
off a vine whose name I did not know.

Five crows held council in an oak tree,
flew away when I approached.
Something has been tearing
the Osage oranges to yellow shreds.

I found a purple leaf and a snail shell.
More I did not accomplish—
besides standing, still, in amazement
at the colors of the cardinals.

The Bluebells

We wandered
into the realm of the bluebells
that dwell in the flood plain
after the spring rains.

Carefully
we stepped
through the blue kingdom.

We could not hear
the tiny bells
ringing with mirth,

but we saw
the great heron lift off
toward the river,
his silent blue-winged shadow
gliding over the flowers.

Vanishing Act

The stream disappears, swallowed
by insatiable karst. We live
on porous land.

Skin deep soil hides the unknown:
passages that worm through earth flesh
open into wombs and cathedrals.
Flowstone gleams wet like mucous membranes.

Water seeps through fractures,
dissolves and deposits.

We must descend deep
to understand
what lies below,
where crystals form
under heat and pressure.

Grown larger, the stream
emerges again down valley,
unexpected.

Ferrying Turtles

On the logs, the turtles dry in the sun:
cooters, map turtles, sliders.
As I approach, they drop, one by one,
into the river and swim away.

A box turtle is swept along,
bobs up and down, helpless,
wiggles her feet and stretches her neck,
trying to keep her head above water.

I reach her with my paddle,
scoop her up—she slides off with a splash
and floats further. Disappears
under a downed tree.

Reappears, struggling downstream.
I overtake her, grab her by the shell,
plop her into my kayak. Ferry her to the shore,
carry her inland to a patch of grass.

She takes off swiftly. No sign
of hesitation or bewilderment.
Some day she may tell the other turtles
about her encounter with God.

The Heron

He looks at the clumsy creatures
in their colorful kayaks
floating down the river.
He can sense their excitement.

In their colorful kayaks,
they gesture and point at him.
He can sense their excitement.
They rest their paddles, drift,

and gesture to be silent.
He lets them come closer.
They rest their paddles, drift
to where he stands on the shore.

When they come closer,
he flies further downriver,
lands on the shore, waits, takes off,
his great wings beating slowly

he flies downstream. He can play
his game with the clumsy creatures.
With slow beats of his great wings
he can fly away. They float down the river.

Stopping by Welch Hospital Ruin

Barred window holes,
giraffe rock walls:
field stones, irregular
in shape and size.

Never a tortured place—
just clean moist air,
failing lungs breathing hope
from the cool cave.

The doctor died.
His project crumbled.
Only ghosts now gasp
in the empty shell.

The spring still gushes
from the underground,
choking cold, the water
still rushes to swell the river.

Orange is the Color of Joy

The lilies in the field
do not toil nor spin—
they work the alchemy

of blooming, distill
sunlight, water, and air
into an orange miracle.

In ditches and fencerows
they flower with abandon,
throats open wide. As summer

fades, the lilies tire.
Willpower cannot halt
the wilting of leaves.

The lilies retreat
to their roots, feed
on sugar stores, dream

of blossoms, emerge
in fierce independence
next year. So it is decreed.

Landmarks

Fog shrouds the river.
Dew collects on leaves,
rolls off in heavy drops.
White asters bloom. The bees

buzz nectar-drunk. Summer
hums a drowsy tune.
Below the calm green spring,
a former mill: a dam,

a rusty turbine—traces
of human work that mar
the landscape. History:
a relay of generations.

The baton itself changes
as it changes hands.

Any Day You See an Eagle Is a Good Day

I have lost something I cannot name.
I go to the river and wait.
Perhaps I will find it. Perhaps
I will learn to do without.

I go to the river and wait.
I have nothing to do but to pay attention.
I will learn to do without
the daily clutter and clamor—

there is nothing to do but to pay attention.
Paying attention is a remedy
for the clutter and clamor in my mind.
I watch a snail on a lobelia lip.

Paying attention is an antidote
for apathy and sadness.
I watch the snail on the lobelia lip,
its translucent shell a perfect spiral,

and forget apathy and sadness.
The wood duck leads her ducklings close to shore.
The snail's shell is a translucent spiral.
The ducks weave through the water willows,

led by their mother, close to shore.
An eagle perches on a sycamore.
The ducklings hide between the water willows.
The eagle sits in silence. He unfolds

his wings and lifts off from the sycamore.
I have forgotten what I had lost—
I saw an eagle, unfolded
my grief, found something I cannot name.

Peace of the River

I want to spend a year by the river
and live in her seasons, wake and sleep
each day to her music, smell her mood.

I would be up early to see the mists
rise from the water and to watch
the great heron wade in the shallows.

I would walk on the banks at dusk
when the shadows lengthen and wait
for the bats to emerge from the cliffs.

I would listen to the muddy torrent
that rages after the winter rains
and warns me to keep my distance

and to her languid green summer voice
that beckons me to throw myself into her arms,
trusting her to carry me past the jungled bluffs.

I would let myself be cleansed and blessed,
the peace of the river would fill my soul,
and I would have to stay forever.

Fallen Stars

Dream-driven, they came
from the East, settled

by the creek
in a valley of promise.

Patient hands piled
river rocks, marked

the homestead—
a testament to hope.

The land shriveled the hope.
Broke the promise.

Briars conquered
the pasture. Shrubs

swallowed the garden,
vines the barn.

Inside the farmhouse
wallpaper scraps,

a broken shelf, the shards
of pink porcelain cups.

The wall remains.
Trees grew up in the gaps.

The low sun slants
a last beam over the stones.

The sweetgum leaves
are fallen stars.

Pioneer Cemetery

The path is overgrown
with river oats and briars.
Few come here.

A row of sandstone slabs,
tinged green by time, tilted
by the weight of decades:

no names, no dates,
no record of lives
faded into history. Only

the oaks stand watch,
and, in the spring, anemones
adorn the ground.

Creation through Subtraction

In the *Economist*,
I read about the cells in the leaves,
the mesophylls that capture
sunlight and air, wisely arranged

veins run through the tree,
the xylem draws water
up from the roots;
the phloem sends sugars
to the tips of the furthest branches.

Come, marvel at the patterns,
the miraculous order:
how following the rules of physics
creates a living being.

I sit by the river
watch the leaves
quiver in the wind,
murmur as if in prayer.
The spirit understands
the archaic language.

Between greening and letting go,
the trees put on a show
as chlorophyll breaks down, leaves
the other colors visible.
Creation through subtraction.

Lectionary

Open the lectionary
of the forest.
Find chapter and verse
for each season,
each moon cycle.

First full moon
after equinox:
read the maples. Consider
their luminous leaves. Observe
the process of letting go.
Feel it deep in your body.

Listen to the wind
preach his sermon.
Hear the yellow grasses rustle.
They know the secret.
So do the bats.

Go to the river.
She whispers words
that are missing
in the dictionary,
roars them in her rapids.

With enough patience,
you can see the wind
whittle the sandstone.
See autumn slide into winter.
Nobody will solve
the riddle for you.

Perhaps the riddle
has no solution.
Perhaps the puzzle box
cannot be opened.

A Forest of Gramophones

The lake is a woodcut,
black and white
wind-carved
zigzag reflections,
the dark silhouette
of the far shore.

In the shallows,
the lotus thrives.
Water beads
on the large round leaves
that float, anchored
to the muddy bottom.

Closer to shore,
the stalks rise higher,
leaves curl
to trumpets, a forest
of gramophones
playing inaudible music—

we only hear
the blue jays shriek
in the distance
and the swish-and-drip
of our paddles.

Passing through the Ozarks

When they had feasted
on the abundant fish
and preened their plumage

with their great beaks,
the pelicans took wing
over the lake,

their sunlit bodies
white before the blue,
their squadron

an undulating ribbon
waved by wind,
swinging higher and higher

and out of sight.

Interruption

The birds scatter.
A large-winged shadow
swoops—

settles on the dead
branch above the feeder.
The hawk surveys the field.

When he flies off, the branch
bounces up and down—
long after he is gone

and the chickadees are already back,
chirping and chattering
as if nothing happened.

O that we may so regroup after peril,
return again and again
to our ordinary lives.

Ephemeral

Frost flowers bloom at the feet
of white crownbeard, only
at the threshold of winter,
before the sap retreats to the roots.

The stalks exhale. Vapor
freezes to ribbons that curl
around pale stems
like bows of blown glass.

White in the morning grass,
the most fleeting of flowers
linger longest
in the deepest shade.

What Stories They Whisper

I have learned to tell sassafras
by its fragrance: it smells
like my grandmother's Eau de Cologne.

Leafless, the trees reveal
their skeletons. The sycamore
reaches her naked arms

over the creek. Oaks clutch
the air with gnarled fingers. My hands
linger on alligator-barked persimmon.

Dry leaves still cling
to the branches. They rustle. Listen—
what stories they whisper!

Destiny

Silver haired, the year
rests in the field.
Crows gather
on the sycamore bones.
The day tastes like glass.
Winter lurks
in the shadows.

In brittle glades
papery pods protect
the last seeds.
Empty coneflowers stand tall;
the goldfinches had their harvest—
everywhere signs of a cycle
fulfilled.

Amy Wright Vollmar

Sycamore
Platanus occidentalis

Photo by Jake Vollmar

Amy Wright Vollmar

As a child I lived in Alton, Illinois, where I discovered the joys of playing in the woods near my home. Deeper in southern Illinois, with my dad's family, I learned how to sing Appalachian folk songs about frogs, dogs, and mules, and how to find hickory nuts along the Little Wabash River. At Monmouth College in Illinois, I majored in English; my professors were afraid that I was going to become a Romantic poet! After a few years in Texas, where I learned to hunt for pecans, fossilized sea urchins, and woolly mammoth tusks, I moved to Springfield, Missouri, with my family.

Hiking, kayaking, and writing helped me learn about the wild Ozarks. In Springfield, I also spent twelve years working with first graders at Phelps Center for Gifted Education. Now retired, I scramble around on the bluffs above the James River in Stone County, Missouri, and try to show people the beautiful fragility of the wild Ozarks through my poetry. Some of these poems have previously appeared in *Cave Region Review* and in *Elder Mountain: A Journal of Ozarks Studies*. My first book of poetry, *Follow*, was published by Cornerpost Press in March of 2020.

When I was young, I haunted the wooded ravine behind my subdivision, with my imaginary mountain lion for company. Soon I learned to bring a notebook with me, to write what I learned about that place. The woods shared poison ivy and mosquitoes, but also gave me fascinating glacier-scratched rocks, spring beauties, and swift creeks to follow. I discovered that blue jays would warn me of snakes, and that I could find peace by listening to the footsteps of wild deer. Years later, when I crossed the Mississippi River to live in Missouri, I brought my notebooks along.

As I write poetry, I'm invariably in motion through the Missouri Ozarks. For me, making poetry is a path to a deeper experience of nature. I often identify with the scarred—but healing—Ozarks landscape of second-growth forest, rivers, and wildlife. Nature recovers in ways that constantly inspire me.

If you want to go poetry-hunting in the Ozarks, follow a path to a forest, hill, waterfall, or river. You will need good hiking sneakers, a small mudproof notebook, and a smudge-resistant pen. I usually wear bug repellant and keep a pocket open for treasures like fossils and lost fishing lures. My kayak is my favorite way to travel by river, but you may prefer a canoe. You must pay attention to field guides, like crows and three-toed box turtles, foxes, and gar. They can show you unexpected ways into the nearby wild. Don't forget to look for owl pellets and rabbit trails. Sniff for sassafras, and taste a blackberry, if you don't mind the sandy seeds.

Make maps in your poems. Discover, listen, stumble, and learn. And don't forget to share—around a campfire, by a fireplace, in a song, a poem or a story. You may guide a hopeful stranger along your trail into the fragile but beautiful landscape of the Ozarks. That stranger may find peace and become your friend.

Signs

I should have turned back
at the place
where the gravel path

washes out with every storm,
but I'd have missed
discoveries—

trillium's unfolding heart,
and mayapple's
hidden flowering,

the tender white
shocked by its own
fierce yellow core—

and this brush
with a wild turkey.
How quietly

it leans,
then slips
into the feathered woods.

Purchase

To own a bluff
maybe
means you will own

a waterfall,
a sycamore where dragonflies
hunt through leaves,

the walnut tree's
rainfall harp strings,
and any feathers

the heron happens
to leave by the river.
You could carve

a road along
the ledges,
build a wall

of limestone.
Or you could climb
now and then

up the waterfall
to the seep
where squirrels drink.

You could watch
for the twin fawns,
look for spearpoints,

and let soft seeds
drift
just past your hands.

Riffle

Down from the waterfall's
broken ledge,

through a sieve
of shell and bone

the river pours,
and at the rim

where small plants drown
above chert flakes

and the roots sip
to slake the bluff,

the shiners flit.
More eye than fin,

new every spring,
these chips of life

flick downstream,
begin.

Verge

In a flow of grasses,
the break
one hoofprint wide
shows us a way

past a gate of thorn.
We turn to learn
how the deer see—
all round, cedars

hold the chill
of the deep hill thicket
where wild plum's lace
draws bumblebees

and branches hold out buds.
Wake robin's silent
but the cardinal
is careless with song

and above,
where the leaves part
the sky spins, blue
as spring water—

crows' wings slip through.
Beyond us
curves the path, still
one hoofprint wide—

just out of sight
the deer shift
among the mayapples
back here.

Secret

Though crows
keep watch
they don't spy me—

from the ridge above
they call
that the waterfall

is safe today—
no deer or bobcat stirs
this cold ravine.

They have left
the waterfall
without a guard,

so I can climb
to a half-moon
of crystal niche

where the water
shapes a channel
below leaves

and broken chert,
speaks through the stone.
Wild grapevines

keep shifting
in their sleep.
And the barred owl's call

resounds
through my own
breathing.

Swallowhole

I'm near the creek
at my own risk,
the signs tell me—

banks could collapse
into the deep,
currents may take

me beyond reach
of hackberry root
down the swallowhole—

where the creek veers
from its safe path
to plunge beneath

the soft clay bank
below my feet,
carrying sky,

tearing a way
through coils of stone,
pulsing down hollow

when it vanishes,
making a cave
I want to see.

Field Guide

Though I've never seen
a sora rail,
life holds

surprises.
Where the river bends
I've found a flint knife,

traced the deep scar
where a bear slid in mud.
Just now I saw

a yellow mayfly
vanish,
become part fish.

A gray squirrel
drinks deeply
from the bitter lake

and the very smallest
of all white moths
darts into my eye!

Blueprint

To make
your own trail
one step wide,

you'll have to pry
rounds of stone
from the forest,

show them how
to become
part of your path.

They will not be
woods or way,
but a border

you create,
so that each time
you want to climb

up the ravine,
you can touch
a certain fern

and the canine teeth
of a possum skull,
or avoid the place

where ticks rain down,
but choose the seep
where hope nibbles

and a toad
in the guise of bark
lifts eyes to you.

Here is a ledge—
you can make a step,
remember your way

to the highest
reach of bluff
where the blue chert

chips away
from sky,
sharp enough

that you won't want
to rearrange
the place you find.

Voices

This waterfall
makes the sound
of a squirrel's teeth

on a hickory nut,
while another
echoes a spring

storm pouring
through the downspouts
of the forest,

rinsing catkins
from the bluff.
Upstream

I've found the waterfall
that a cave's jug
tips to let spill

into the river—
but only one
waterfall

is the stir of air
pushed by wings
of the great blue

heron
as she lifts
from stone—

only one.

Gooseberry

I slit its misty
raindrop globe

and count white seeds
that brighten

while I watch—
nothing within

this liquid orb
is wholly sweet

or spitting sour—
only green

and mostly seed.
One bite—

I slip through
skin of thorn

along bright leaves
through the windowpanes

of my planet,
seize light

in my teeth,
and tear.

Noland Hollow

On my map
this river
is a gooseneck in blue

on an even page,
but inside
the map

the river is green
and thick with seeds,
sycamore leaves

and limestone dust.
The inky lines
of the old bluff

tear and blur
where cedars cling—
they break

into caves
and dens—
so on my way

downstream
I follow only
the geese,

who leave a trail
of feather curls
as they veer

into autumn
with the river,
swerving round

a curve of bluff
I cannot place
on any map.

Directions

If you walk
near the waterfall

do not worry,
though you may slip

on a bitten
persimmon,

tumble
over a limestone ledge

or disappear
beneath sycamore leaves—

along this shifting bluff
there is not one

clear way
to find the river.

Spark

The waterfall
is asleep now,
so I can sit

in her knobby lap
among the roots
of poison ivy,

feel her holding me
in her cool pocket
with a tumble

of sorted chert
and speckled leaves.
I listen—

within the bluff,
beneath the dry
worn rifts

in the limestone,
inside caves
where crystal's bite

reminds me
she's still alive,
I hear her broken chords—

she is breathing.

Crow Moon

I've read that hedgeapples
fed the mammoths
before this creek

ran warm—
now deer will nibble
the tarry pulp

only in times
of winter need.
I think this vein

of creekbank woods
was meant for crows—
all in the sycamore

branches they sway,
warn me away
from the red ribcage

and the beak-torn eyes
of the coyotes' deer—
but at times

this is a place
I need to pick
apart and swallow.

North Arrow

Snowmelt droplets
slip through stone,
down to the creek

where the current
gulps at sun,
pushes it through

a spine of rock
to wake the flesh
of blackberry roots,

and an owl tells me—
though my sycamore perch
has peeled to ice,

rabbits are frail
and mouseribs show—
still these creekbank woods

are home.

Cold Snap

At twelve degrees
my path's a hull
over the bluff

but the waterfall
is running still,
alive

where sun
gnaws ribs of ice,
picking through leaves,

scratching at clay,
cracking chert
to shell crystals.

The oaks have sealed
their buds against
the cold,

but cedars flit
with quavers
of titmice

who whistle
up the hollow,
calling for spring

to unlock
the gates of ice,
open these woods.

Passage

In deep winter
you can brave thorns
to find

a sinkhole—
follow deer trails
until your daylight

bounds away,
then slip into
the forest's sigh

where wild grapevines
hold limestone still
amidst its spill

into a hollow
that draws woodsmoke,
torn oak boughs,

the sparrow's song
and your breath
down to misted

quiet.

Crow Song

Crows shake
the locust thorns,

break through the sky,
make their own paths

along the creek.
Above cedar boughs

all split by ice,
over even sycamores

they tumble, swing
through blue

along the border
of the prairie.

Their lives whirl
over mine,

throw no shadows.
Here in the thicket

I'm in dusk
among the thorns.

Oh, to glide
above the creek

in early spring
on another's wings,

and still know a name
for me.

To the Waterfall in Winter

If there is no path,
create one—
on deer-hoof feet

crush leaves, pause
while your ears twitch
and you scan

the limestone ridge
you're following—
the black caves listen.

Then slide three times
on leaf-hidden stones
and so blunder at last

to the waterfall—
sit on a rock so slant
that you're leaning over

a ledge-trickle, a pool
of wet chert gravel
with oak-leaf drain.

The water slips, drips,
chains, snaps
over rock and moss

that's the palest of greens,
a bobcat's eyes
peering through twigs.

You may never know
what inside you
needs healing,

but when the sedge wren
lights on the vine
at the base of your rock

and you feel every speckle
of her feathers,
her pine needle feet,

her vivid eyes
trusting you,
you'll trust yourself

to climb, if you like
as high as the cave
up there, by the sky

where the waterfall starts—
a cave too small
for your shoulders—

but through limestone
pierced by rain
for how many years

hear how the waterfall
begins—
one drop.

Then, If Ever

This sycamore, a bridge
that doesn't cross
the river,

still lets us lean through shade
over the light,
the song

that pours to us from roots
and rocks above.
The trills

of water, warbler—all we hear—
as we perch
on roots,

the mended patchwork of
the sycamore's lap.
We sit,

sip water, jump to skim
limestones, to see
flit-minnows

and a damselfly—so turquoise
of tail, cobalt
of wing

on her leaf she is—
we cannot say
how lovely.

Sanders Spring

So many ways
through the bluff

water knows—
how to pass

through sinkhole
and chains

of lightless stone,
to channel

beneath roots and dens,
and then to rise,

speaking
the language

of the waterthrush,
and pour

to make the story
of these woods.

Stray

Wind along the bluff
chimes high
in the sycamores,

wheezes through
the slots of caves
and the throats

of chickadees,
stirs the dead asters.
Something comes

bounding, with golden seeds
and thorns woven
through its fur,

to rub a cold blue
muzzle against my hand,
follow me home.

The Oven Bird

There is a singer everyone has heard,
Loud, a mid-summer and a mid-wood bird,
Who makes the solid tree trunks sound again.
He says that leaves are old and that for flowers
Mid-summer is to spring as one to ten.
He says the early petal-fall is past
When pear and cherry bloom went down in showers
On sunny days a moment overcast;
And comes that other fall we name the fall.
He says the highway dust is over all.
The bird would cease and be as other birds
But that he knows in singing not to sing.
The question that he frames in all but words
Is what to make of a diminished thing.

Robert Frost

ACKNOWLEDGMENTS

The authors wish the thank the publishers of the following books and journals in which some of these poems appeared.

C. D. Albin
"Axe, Fire, Mule" *Concho River Review*; *Axe, Fire, Mule*
"Burial Oak" (unpublished)
"The Cellar" (unpublished)
"Cicero Jack Considers the Cougar's Return" *The Cape Rock*; *Axe, Fire, Mule*
"Cicero Jack, Farmer, Rues the Ruin of an Ozark River" *Moon City Review*; *Axe, Fire, Mule*
"Glaucoma" *The Cape Rock*; *Axe, Fire, Mule*
"Here and Now" *Cave Region Review*; *Axe, Fire, Mule*
"Intruder" *Mid-America Poetry Review*; *Axe, Fire, Mule*
"The Neighbor" (unpublished)
"Notice of Sale" *Cave Region Review*
"Origin Stories" *Elder Mountain*
"Ozark Dark" *Cave Region Review*; *Axe, Fire, Mule*
"Pharaoh Dreamed of Cattle" *Cave Region Review*; *Axe, Fire, Mule*
"Provenance" *Cave Region Review*
"The Subterfuge of Stones" (unpublished)
"Testament" *Mid-America Poetry Review*
"White-Tail" *Big Muddy*; *Axe, Fire, Mule*
"The Will and Testament of Cicero Jack" *The Cape Rock*; *Axe, Fire, Mule*

Wendy Taylor Carlisle
"August: An Ozark Sonnet" as "August: Arkansas" *The Mercy of Traffic*
"Bees" *The Dead Mule School of Southern Literature*
"Blossom" *The Mercy of Traffic*
"Buck Mountain" *The Mercy of Traffic*
"Catch and Release" *Discount Fireworks*
"Cold Time: An Ozark Sonnet" *Red Wolf Journal: Coronavirus Issue*
"Come and Gone" as "Early September" *Rat's Ass Review*
"Cuts" *Cider Press Review*
"Dream" *Chapbook Number 8* in Platypus Press Series
"Inspiration" (unpublished)

"Kings River" (unpublished)
"Naked" *Reading Berryman to the Dog*
"NEST: An Ozark Sonnet" *Rat's Ass Review*
"Ode" (unpublished)
"OK to Burn" *The Mercy of Traffic*
"Provision" (unpublished)
"Rumor" *The Mercy of Traffic*
"Smudged" as "Forecast" *The Mercy of Traffic*
"Snow" *Global Poemic*
"Spell: An Ozark Sonnet" *Heron Tree*
"Turkey Buzzard" *Gyroscope*
"Undress" *Dairy Hollow Echo*
"Up Here We Make Our Own Darkness" *On the Way to the Promised
    Land Zoo*
"Weather" *Blue Lake Review*
"We Walk the Trail More Slowly" (Unpublished)

Paulette Guerin
"Beads of sleet" (unpublished)
"Bluest" (unpublished)
"Cabin in the Ozarks" (unpublished)
"Childhood" *Elder Mountain*; *Wading through Lethe*
"Diminuendo" *Empty House Press*; *Wading through Lethe*
"Emily Dickinson Floats the Buffalo River" *Sixfold*
"End of Autumn" (unpublished)
"The Far Side of the Mountain" *Orson's Review*; *Wading through Lethe*
"First Communion" *Sixfold*; *Wading through Lethe*
"Ginkgo" *Cantos*; *Wading through Lethe*
"Goodbye" (unpublished)
"In the Ozarks" (unpublished)
"Mercy" *The Concho River Review*; *Wading through Lethe*
"Mountain Air" *Elder Mountain*; *Wading through Lethe*
"Night Out at Cadron Creek Catfish House, Choctaw, Arkansas" *Elder
    Mountain*
"Old Trees" (unpublished)
"One summer" (unpublished)
"Owl" *Elder Mountain*
"Parasite" (unpublished)
"Roots" *Wading Through Lethe*
"Signs" *SLANT: A Journal of Poetry*
"Summer, Greers Ferry Lake" *Elder Mountain*; *Wading through Lethe*

"Visit" (unpublished)
"Weaving" (unpublished)
"Winter Hike" (unpublished)

John J. Han
"Arkansas: Travel Haiku" *Fireflies' Light*
"An Autumn Evening" *Spare Mule*
"Autumn Haiku" *Geppo*
"Autumn in the Ozarks: Haiku" *Elder Mountain*
"Autumn Squirrels: Haiku" *Heart Breaths: Book of Contemporary Haiku*
"Cat Haiku" *Cave Region Review*
"Deepening Autumn" *Cave Region Review*
"Departing Autumn" *The Plover and the Moonstone*
"Four Seasons: Tanka" *Cave Region Review*
"The Lake of the Ozarks" *Elder Mountain*
"Living Under the Shadow of Death" (unpublished)
"A Nightly Encounter" *Cave Region Review*
"On a Spring Morning" *The Plover and the Moonstone*
"Ozark Beauty: Haiku" *Cave Region Review*
"Sights and Sounds of Winter" *Valley Voices*
"Smitten with the Hills" *Spare Mule*
"Snapshots of Summer: Haiku"
        "summer breeze" *Modern Haiku*
        "corn tassels" *Geppo*
        "Father's Day" *Geppo*
        "cicadas" *Geppo*
        "the lover cat" *Geppo*
        "summer night" *Geppo*
"Snapshots of Winter: Haiku"
        "all that remains" *Geppo*
        "winter encounter" *Geppo*
        "winter woods" *Geppo*
        "winter river" *Geppo*
        "winter wind" *Mariposa*
"Spring Haiku"
        "clifftop in springtime" *Visiting the Wind*
        "coming of spring" *Geppo*
        "only because" *Chrysanthemum*
        "spring meadow" and "spring wind" *Geppo*
        "April" *Modern Haiku*
"Spring Rain" *Taj Mahal Review*

"Springtime Japanese Garden" *Spare Mule*
"Spring 2020: Haiku" *Taj Mahal Review*
"Squirrels Gone Wild" *Spare Mule*
"The Sunny Spot" (unpublished)
"Where Does the Ozarks Begin?" *Spare Mule*
"Winter Haiku" *Cave Region Review*
"Winter Mountain: Haiku" *Elder Mountain*

Phillip Howerton
"Barn Removal" *Intégrité: A Faith and Learning Journal*
"Barn Swallows" *Elder Mountain*
"Bloodroot" *The Ozarks Mountaineer*; *The History of Tree Roots*
"Farm Journal: Haiku Sequence" *The History of Tree Roots*
      "barn door—" *Bear Creek haiku*
      "bullfrog" *South by Southwest*
      "falling through" *The Ozarks Mountaineer*
      "heat wave—" *Brussels Sprout*
      "heron and I" *Brussels Sprout*
      "in my mailbox" *Haiku Headlines*
      "i turn out my lamp" *Frogpond*
      "new moon," *Brussels Sprout*
      "old pony—" *The Ozarks Mountaineer*
      "out of the city" *Haiku Headlines*
      "setting early" *The Ozarks Mountaineer*
      "shifting fog" *Brussels Sprout*
      "snake in the shed" *Brussels Sprout*
      "walking back" *Black Bough*
      "wild ivy" *Brussels Sprout*
"The Farm Youth's Companion" *Elder Mountain*
"The Fencerow" *Journal of Kentucky Studies*; *The History of Tree Roots*
"Gods of Four Mile Creek" (unpublished)
"The History of Tree Roots" *Elder Mountain*; *The History of Tree Roots*
"Mayapple" *Cave Region Review*; *The History of Tree Roots*
"Mayflies in the Foyer of a Nursing Home" *Cave Region Review*
"On a Bluff Overlooking the Buffalo National River" *OzarksWatch*;
      The History of Tree Roots
"On Her Blindness" *Ozarks Alive, Plainsongs*
"Opossum" *Offerings*; *The History of Tree Roots*
"Persimmon Tree at Leyda and Summit" *Elder Mountain*
"Prickly Pear" *The Midwest Quarterly*
"Rain Crow" *Pegasus*; *The History of Tree Roots*

"The Redbuds" (unpublished)
"To Know This Place" (unpublished)
"September 15" *Cantos*
"Small Bluets" *Timber Creek Review*; *The History of Tree Roots*
"Turkey Buzzards" *Cantos*
"While Cleaning the Shed" (unpublished)
"Whippoorwill" *Elder Mountain*; *The History of Tree Roots*
"Wild Cherry Trees" (unpublished)

Gerry Sloan
"Assisi is Everywhere" *Cantos*
"Centipede" *Crossings: A Memoir in Verse*
"Danzón" *Cave Region Review*
"Double Exposure" *Elder Mountain*
"The Fox" *Paper Lanterns*
"Grandmother Gourd" *Cantos*
"Greenhouse Addendum" *Thirteen*; *Paper Lanterns*
"Howl for Susan Powell" *Elder Mountain*
"Layers" *Paper Lanterns*
"Nature Channel" *Paper Lanterns*
"Ode Ending with a Line by Roethke" *Cave Region Review*
"Osage Orange" *Crossings: A Memoir in Verse*
"Poem at the Solstice" *Cave Region Review*
"Rock-Skipping on the West Fork" *Alura Quarterly*; *Old Hickory Review*; *Along the River: An Anthology of Contemporary Arkansas Poetry*; *Paper Lanterns*
"Shadows of Mount Sequoyah" (unpublished)
"The Star That Got Its Wish" *Paper Lanterns*
"Swallows" *Cave Region Review*
"Thaw" (unpublished)
"Why France Sold Us Louisiana" *Cave Region Review*
"Windows" *Tipton Poetry Journal*

Mark Spitzer
"Big Al: The Name Remains" *Cryptozarkia*
"Goggle-Eye Gobbledygook" *Cryptozarkia*
Excerpts from "GLURK!" from *GLURK! A Hellbender Odyssey*
"Mythology of The Terrible Green Gowrow" *Crypto-Arkansas*
"Old Blue Possibilities" *Cryptozarkia*

Agnes Vojta
"Any Day You See an Eagle Is a Good Day" (unpublished)
"The Bluebells" *Porous Land*
"Burning Brush" (unpublished)
"Celebrating the Thaw" (unpublished)
"Creation through Subtraction" *A Coracle for Dreams*
"Destiny" *Porous Land*
"Ephemeral" *Porous Land*
"Fallen Stars" as "Stone Wall in the Ozarks" in *A Coracle for Dreams*
"Ferrying Turtles" *Bindweed Magazine*; *A Coracle for Dreams*
"A Forest of Gramophones" (unpublished)
"The Heron" (unpublished)
"Interruption" (unpublished)
"Landmarks" (unpublished)
"Lectionary" *A Coracle for Dreams*
"Orange is the Color of Joy" (unpublished)
"Passing through the Ozarks" (unpublished)
"Peace of the River" *The Eden of Perhaps*
"Pioneer Cemetery" (unpublished)
"Status Report" *Gyroscope Magazine*; *A Coracle for Dreams*
"Stopping by Welch Hospital Ruin" (unpublished)
"Vanishing Act" *Porous Land*
"What Stories They Whisper" (unpublished)
"Witch Hazel" *A Coracle for Dreams*

Amy Wright Vollmar
"Blueprint" (unpublished)
"Cold Snap" (unpublished)
"Crow Moon" *Cave Region Review*; *Follow*
"Crow Song" *Cave Region Review*; *Follow*
"Directions" (unpublished)
"Field Guide" *Cave Region Review*; *Follow*
"Gooseberry" (unpublished)
"Noland Hollow" *Elder Mountain*; *Follow*
"North Arrow" *Cave Region Review*; *Follow*
"Passage" (unpublished)
"Purchase" *Elder Mountain*; *Follow*
"Riffle" *Cave Region Review*; *Follow*
"Sanders Spring" (unpublished)
"Secret" (unpublished)
"Signs" *Cave Region Review*; *Follow*

"Spark" (unpublished)
"Stray" *Cave Region Review*; *Follow*
"Swallowhole" *Elder Mountain*
"Then, If Ever" *Cave Region Review*; *Follow*
"To the Waterfall in Winter" *Cave Region Review*; *Follow*
"Verge" *Cave Region Review*; *Follow*
"Voices" *Cave Region Review*; *Follow*

About the Editor

Phillip Howerton holds a PhD in American literature and rhetoric and composition from the University of Missouri-Columbia. His essays, reviews, and poems have appeared in numerous journals and books. He is a co-founder and co-editor of *Cave Region Review*, general editor of *Elder Mountain: A Journal of Ozarks Studies*, and founder and owner of Cornerpost Press. His poetry collection, *The History of Tree Roots*, was published by Golden Antelope Press in 2015, and his survey of Ozarks literature, *The Literature of the Ozarks: An Anthology*, was published by University of Arkansas Press in February of 2019, a project for which he received the 2019 Missouri Literary Award from the Missouri Library Association.